THE GOD OF GLORY

THE GOD OF GLORY

GARY McBRIDE

THE GOD OF GLORY
By: Gary McBride
Copyright © 2015
GOSPEL FOLIO PRESS
All Rights Reserved

Published by Gospel Folio Press
304 Killaly St. West Port Colborne ON L3K 6A6

ISBN: 9781927521755

Cover design by Danielle Robins

All Scripture quotations from the
King James Version unless otherwise noted.

Scripture taken from the New King James Version®. Copyright © 1982 by Thomas Nelson, Inc. Used by permission. All rights reserved.

Scripture taken from the Holy Bible, NEW INTERNATIONAL VERSION®. Copyright © 1973, 1978, 1984 by Biblica, Inc. All rights reserved worldwide. Used by permission.

Scripture quotations are taken from the Holy Bible, New Living Translation, copyright ©1996, 2004, 2007 by Tyndale House Foundation. Used by permission of Tyndale House Publishers, Inc., Carol Stream, Illinois 60188. All rights reserved.

Printed in Canada

FOREWORD

*Wonderful the matchless grace of Jesus,
Deeper than the mighty rolling sea;*

• • •

*His love has no limits; His grace has no measure,
His power no boundary known unto men;*

• • •

*O the deep, deep love of Jesus, vast, unmeasured, boundless, free!
Rolling as a mighty ocean in its fullness over me!*

• • •

Precious thoughts from the innumerable hymns written about our God and Redeemer present the immeasurable vastness of His grace and love. These are only a few of the attributes of His glorious character; Scripture conveys that there are even more. It will require the unending duration of eternity to reveal His all in all, *"that in the ages to come He might show the exceeding riches of His grace"* (Eph. 2:7, NKJV).

The glory of God in simplest terms is the expression of His person and character, a subject too broad to fully grasp. To contemplate for a moment that a book of this size could convey all that we can know of the glory of God would be an offense to its subject. To read these pages is only to be introduced to the glorious splendor of who God is and what He has done. It will stir your heart to give Him the glory due His name. This topic should be of importance to us when we consider that we were created for His glory (Isa. 43:7).

To those who have enjoyed the privilege of hearing Gary minister or have read his previous writings, it is clear that he is a man with a deep appreciation for what the Lord has done for him. That appreciation fuels Gary's passion to know more of the Lord with the express purpose of being able to encourage God's people. Gary's messages, writing, and conversation have always been characterized by a practical simplicity through which he conveys the truth of Scripture. Such simplicity can only be achieved as a result of a firm grasp of the living Word acquired through diligent study and prayerful meditation. The reader will appreciate being able to share in the bounty of devotional thoughts Gary has reaped from his reflections on the God of glory.

Having contemplated the pages of this manuscript several times, I liken them to a large tapestry hanging from a museum wall. An initial viewing unveils unique portions that snatch the mind's attention and stir the heart to ponder the manners in which the glory of God is revealed. Inherent in each chapter are captivating perspectives of the glory of God, which can be enjoyed in an isolated reading of the chapter. However, upon each rereading, new portions will be highlighted and God's splendor magnified. The reader is given cause to step back and appreciate in some small measure the tapestry of God's glory woven together by the threads of the Son's glory. Every individual aspect of God is glorious, but a panoramic view of God's character transitions one's focus to the united glory of God as revealed both in His work and in His person.

Be assured that considering the glories of Him who will one day reign eternally in all glory is time well spent.

David J. Reed
St. Catharines, Ontario

PREFACE

The production of this book has been a process. This manuscript started as a series of messages given at a family camp at Galilee Bible Camp in Renfrew, Ontario. From there, they morphed into a series of articles published in Precious Seed magazine. The next step is now in your hand in the form of a book.

To develop a series of six messages involves a lot of time and effort, but the written notes are mostly a series of points and a few illustrations. Spoken messages can be modified — material added or subtracted — as the Holy Spirit brings other thoughts to mind or the attention of the audience indicates a change of direction is needed. Several pages of notes contain enough material for 45 minutes of ministry.

To produce articles of some 1,700 words is a step beyond sermon notes. Rules of grammar must be followed, repetitious words avoided, clichés and idioms dropped, and attention given to tenses. The subject must be addressed in such a way as to engage the reader, to educate, to edify, and to encourage. In a relatively small amount of space the topic has to be introduced, developed, and finally applied.

The process of writing a book is a little more daunting. The articles in Precious Seed totalled less than 30 typewritten pages. A book is more than double that size. More research is required and quotations need to be referenced with proper credit given. The topic at hand can be addressed more extensively and arranged differently.

I have enjoyed each step of the journey: preparing and presenting the messages; writing the articles; and finally presenting the material in a book. It was never my intention when I first looked at the topic of the glory of God that it would end up in this format. I must say it has been a journey of discovery and delight as I have contemplated this wonderful subject.

There are countless books on this topic by more accomplished writers, penned by men who are of greater depth and who have more spiritual insight than I. Men of greater learning and scholarship could likely communicate these truths in a clearer and more articulate way than I can. With these things in mind, I have tried to produce a book that is different than others on the same topic and in a style that is unique to me. This volume is purposely not very large or wordy, taking into consideration that fewer people take time to read and that those who do are more likely to read something small or short.

Each chapter contains nuggets from God's Word that I have gleaned over the years from the ministry of others, either in preaching or in print. These are truths that I would not have known in my early twenties but have gleaned over time. To more mature readers these thoughts may appear as things you have always known, but remember that you too had to learn them somewhere along the way.

At the end of each chapter I have included a section called "Meditative Thoughts." My rational is that the blessed man of Psalm 1 meditates on the Word of God. The imperative in Colossians 3 is that the Word of Christ dwell in us richly. The key to enjoying fellowship with the God of peace as stated in Philippians 4 is to think on things that are pure and virtuous. These devotional thoughts are included with the hope that they would lead readers to worship—to give glory to God.

To produce a readable manuscript must of necessity involve others. Roy Hill was instrumental in getting the material into *Precious Seed* where John Bennett graciously edited the submissions. From there Sam Cairns encouraged me to publish the material in book form.

I owe a debt of gratitude to David Reed for all of the work he has done on the manuscript. He analysed it and advised

PREFACE

changes, he critiqued and criticised where needed, and he encouraged and helped the project along. His work in the field of electrical engineering equipped him to analyse the material and put it into a flow chart. His work appears in that form at the end of the book and is a product of his enjoyment of the glory of God. He also graciously agreed to write the foreword to this book and I am thankful for that and for the friendship of David and Joanne over many years.

My brother-in-law, Nat Reed, has also put his expertise into this work. He has challenged thoughts and expressions, and edited and formatted the material. I am grateful for his help and encouragement in this endeavor.

As with my other books, the Gospel Folio Press staff have been most helpful. Especially Danielle Robins who has the task of formatting the material, producing the cover, and overseeing the project.

It goes without saying that a book on this topic is written for the glory of God. If His people are encouraged and are drawn to consider this great theme, the book will have served its purpose.

TABLE OF CONTENTS

INTRODUCTION
  The God of Glory 13
CHAPTER ONE:
  Glory Defined and Demonstrated 19
CHAPTER TWO:
  Show Me Your Glory 35
CHAPTER THREE:
  Visions of God's Glory 45
CHAPTER FOUR:
  We Beheld His Glory 57
CHAPTER FIVE:
  The Glory of His Grace 69
CHAPTER SIX:
  Give God Glory 81
CHAPTER SEVEN:
  He Shall Bear the Glory 89
CHAPTER EIGHT:
  To God Be the Glory 99
APPENDIX:
  Sermon Outlines 107
BIBLIOGRAPHY 109
CHART:
  Glory Through the Ages .... back of book

INTRODUCTION

THE GOD OF GLORY

The sum total of all that God is and does, His character, His conduct, and His attributes, could be referred to as the "glory of God." This is the great theme of the ages and ultimately stands as the reason for all that God does. It surpasses creation, revelation, and salvation as the highest motivation for the activities of the Godhead.

The declarations of the Lord in Isaiah 42:8 and 48:11 state, *"My glory I will not give to another"* and *"I will not give My glory unto another"* (NKJV). These statements are made in the context of God's dealings with His people and were given as an answer to idolatry. The Lord will not share His praise with idols; as the second commandment indicates, God is jealous of His glory in the best sense of the word.

John de Silva, in his book, *My Lord and My God*, presents three marks of deity.[1]

- God's attributes determine what only God can do.
- God's prerogative defines what only God can choose to do.
- God's glory declares what only God has done.

He goes on to say that "the glory of God, the wonder and majesty of His Being can be viewed in terms of His exclusive works."[2] The manifestation of this glory is seen in God's work in creation, referred to as His creatorial glory.

---

[1] John W. de Silva, *My Lord and My God* (Kilmarnock: John Ritchie, 2003), 46
[2] ibid., 47

De Silva adds, "There is also however, His unique personal glory—that which is in regard to His essential Being—who and what He is."

DECLARING GLORY

The display of God's glory is the prime reason for the **creation** as seen in the following references. According to Romans 1:19-20, God's invisible attributes, the greatness and majesty that constitute His glory, are visible in and through His creation. In Psalm 19:1 the greatness of God is seen in that *"the heavens declare the glory of God."* This perhaps explains the immeasurable vastness and expanse of the universe. Twice the Psalms declare that God's glory is above the heavens (Ps. 8:1; 113:4), and in Psalm 148:13 His glory is said to be *"above the earth and heaven."* The Psalmist goes on to say, *"His name alone is exalted"* (NKJV).

It is no wonder that Christians everywhere enjoy singing.

> *O Lord my God! When I in awesome wonder*
> *Consider all the works Thy hands have made,*
> *I see the stars; I hear the rolling thunder,*
> *Thy power throughout the universe displayed.*
> *Then sings my soul, my Savior God, to Thee,*
> *How great Thou art! How great Thou art!*
> Translastion by S. Hine

Everything was created by the Lord and for His pleasure. For this reason He is worthy to receive *"glory and honour and power"* (Rev. 4:11). The creation of every person is specifically said to be for His glory (Isa. 43:7).

Not only creation but **redemption** is also *"To the praise of the glory of his grace"* (Eph. 1:6). The whole plan of salvation was designed in such a way that no person would ever be able to boast of their part in the process. It was not and is not a result of merit, works, or self-righteousness but all of faith. If anyone boasts or glories they must glory in the Lord (1 Cor. 1:31).

INTRODUCTION

The person of God and our perception of His person are intimately associated with His glory. He is called **"the God of glory"** both in Acts 7:2 and in Psalm 29:3. In the book of Acts Stephen begins his discourse saying, *"The God of glory appeared to our father Abraham when he was in Mesopotamia"* (Acts 7:2, NKJV). Abraham started his journey with both a glimpse of the glory of God and of the God of glory.

Psalm 29 has been called "The Psalm of the Seven Thunders" as it depicts a storm coming inland from the Mediterranean Sea. Seven times *"the voice of the LORD"* is mentioned in the Psalm. Verse 3 says *"the God of glory thunders"* (NKJV), a reference to an awesome display of His glory in nature. God's people are called upon to give Him the glory that is due to His name.

A similar formula to the phrase **"the God of glory"** is used with each member of the Trinity. This in itself is a strong defence for the doctrine of the Trinity in light of the references already given. In Ephesians 1:17 we read, *"the **Father** of glory."* 1 Corinthians 2:8 speaks of the Son of God, *"the **Lord** of glory."* In 1 Peter 4:14 the Holy Spirit is called *"the **spirit** of glory."* Psalm 24 mentions *"the **King** of glory"* four times as it looks forward to the revelation and reign of Christ. Glory is also presented in association with the person of the Lord as "the glory of God" or "the glory of the Lord."

James 2:1 refers to the Lord Jesus Christ as *"the Lord of glory."* In the KJV, the use of italics for "Lord" indicates the word is not found in the original Greek text. A. T. Robertson in his book *Word Pictures in the New Testament* indicates the proper translation would be "the Glory." He further comments, "James thus terms our Lord Jesus Christ, as the Shekinah Glory of God."[3]

God's glory is prominent in the Old Testament in His dealings with Israel. The visible display of glory was the evidence of His presence with them. F. A. Tatford in his book entitled,

---

3 A. T. Robertson, *Word Pictures in the New Testament* (Nashville: Broadman Press, 1932), 27

What Think Ye of Christ, quotes the following from a Jewish Rabbi: "Where two are seated together, intent on the Torah, glory (Jehovah) is in the midst of them."[4] Rabbis considered "glory" a synonym for the very presence of God.

In the New Testament, and thus in the current age, God's glory has to do with His presence in us, both individually and collectively. For believers it also has to do with His provision for us and His protection of us. For the unsaved world it has to do with His power and His position which will be on display at His second coming to earth.

DEFINING GLORY

"Glory" in common usage refers to "honour," "admiration," or possibly "renown." The word may be used of someone or something that the world considers to be awesome or having extraordinary beauty. The biblical use of the word includes these ideas, but there is more to the word than the world would understand or appreciate.

Even within Christendom, where the word is widely used, most people find it a difficult word to define. This is true though it occurs in many hymns and is often used in prayer. The word "glory" occurs close to 400 times in the Bible and can be found in about 370 verses.

DEMONSTRATING GLORY

God's glory is visible in His creation and through His purposes. In the Old Testament, God's glory was on display in both the Tabernacle and the Temple. There were also individuals in the Old Testament who had personal encounters with the glory of God.

In the New Testament, glory is associated with the person and work of Jesus Christ. There is the glory of His person, of His power, of His passion, and of His position. The Lord Jesus

---

[4] F. A. Tatford, *What Think Ye of Christ*, (Walterick Printing Co. n.d.)

INTRODUCTION

has inherent glory and acquired glory. Our salvation is to His glory and the church is to proclaim His glory.

One of the themes associated with glory in the Scripture is that when God's presence is in view His glory fills the place or the person. Both heaven and earth are full of His glory as were the Tabernacle and the Temple. There was "fullness" in Christ and there should be as well in God's people as well. When God's glory resides within a believer, it becomes visible without.

There is a very practical flow to the revelation of God's glory. God has revealed His glory through His works of creation and redemption. This might be called declarative glory, displaying what is hidden and unseen in order to reveal His essential glory. The Word of God is designed to reveal His glory; for believers today that is where His essential glories are seen.

Glory is also reflected in people who witnessed it, as they were affected by it. The response of God's people should be to render Him glory, the worship due His name. Ultimately all that belongs to Him—including us—is to radiate His glory.

The chart at the back of the book expresses in a visual format a detailed overview of God's glory as revealed through the ages.

CHAPTER ONE
GLORY DEFINED AND DESCRIBED

For any exhaustive word study, observing the occurrences and various ways a word is used is fundamental to our understanding of its meaning. Sound exegesis starts with a definition based on the meaning intended by the various writers of Scripture and as understood by the readers. A major principle of biblical interpretation is the "law of first mention." God introduces places and people, doctrines and concepts, in a way that sets the stage for further usage. For many of these people and concepts, the final mention in Scripture can prove to be enlightening as well.

GLORY IN THE OLD TESTAMENT

In the Old Testament "glory" conveys the thought of "splendor," "beauty," or of someone or something being "awesome." Millard J. Erickson, in his book *Christian Theology*, writes that a number of Hebrew words are translated into our English word "glory." The primary word for "glory" in Hebrew refers to "a perceptible attribute, an individual's display of splendor, wealth and pomp. When used with respect to God it does not point to one particular attribute, but to the greatness of His entire nature."

Strong's Concordance lists the Hebrew words that are translated as "glory" in English. Some of these have to do with man's estimation of himself, as in bragging or seeking glory.

THE GOD OF GLORY

On the positive side the words can mean "beauty," "majesty," or "honour" and can refer to the act of "commending" or "giving praise." As a noun, glory can be rendered "weight" or "splendor." As an adjective it is translated "rich," "severe," "heavy," "weighty," "great," or "glorious."

The Hebrew word contains the idea of "weight" but only in a positive sense. Used in reference to God, it is the sum of all His attributes. Glory has been defined as, "the weightiness of all He possesses in His being."

Charles Ryrie notes that the primary Hebrew word for "glory" carries the thought of something or someone being "awesome" or "important." When the glory of God is seen, it is a revelation of His splendor or importance. Ryrie also points out that when God reveals His glory there is never anything impure or prideful about it.

> God's "glory" is how we describe the sum effect of all His attributes. Such as, grace, truth, goodness, mercy, justice, knowledge, power, eternity—all that He is. Therefore, the glory of God is intrinsic, that is as essential to God as light is to the sun, as blue is to the sky, as wet is to water. You don't make the sun light, it is light. You don't make the sky blue, it is blue. You don't make water wet it is wet. In all of these cases, the attribute is intrinsic to the object.
>
> In contrast, man's glory is granted to him. If you take a king and remove all his robes and crown and give him only a rag to wear and leave him on the streets for a few weeks, when put next to a beggar you'll never know which is which. That is because there is no intrinsic glory. The only glory the king has is when you give him a crown and a robe and sit him on his throne. He has no intrinsic glory.

GLORY DEFINED AND DESCRIBED

That is the point. The only glory that men have is granted to them. The glory that is God's is His in His essence. You cannot de-glory God because glory is His nature. You cannot touch His glory. It cannot be taken away. It cannot be added to. It is His being.[5]

Essential glory is that in God which is glorious—His character which demands honour, worship, and adoration. His **declarative glory** is the showing forth or the revealing of the glory of His character to his creatures, the laying open of His glory. This is what Moses desired—that God would reveal Himself to his mind so that he might know Him—so that he might have a clear and powerful apprehension of those things which constitute God's glory.

The following are some Old Testament examples of the use of the word "glory":

- In Genesis 46:13 Joseph could speak of the glory of His power and position.
- Psalm 19:1 states, *"The heavens declare the glory of God."*
- Psalm 97 speaks of the praise that is to ascend to the Sovereign Lord while anticipating the future reign of Christ: *"The heavens declare his righteousness, and all the peoples see his glory"* (v. 6).

In a number of the Psalms, the theme of glory is prominent as God's people are called upon to give Him glory. This is seen, for instance, in Psalm 96:8, *"Give to the LORD the glory due His name"* (NKJV). Another example can be found in Psalm 29:1-2, *"Give unto the LORD, O you mighty ones, Give unto the LORD glory and strength. Give unto the LORD the glory due to His name; Worship the LORD in the beauty of holiness"* (NKJV). The concept of ascribing worth to God is prevalent throughout the Psalms even when the word "glory" is not used. To praise Him and to lift up His name is to give Him glory.

---

5 Michael P. Green, *Illustrations for Biblical Preaching* (Grand Rapids: Baker Book House)

THE GOD OF GLORY

GOD'S GLORY IN ISRAEL (THE PAST)

IN THEIR TRAVELS

The Israelites witnessed the glory of the Lord with them following their escape from the land Egypt. When Moses went up the mountain to receive the Law in Exodus 24, God's glory covered the mount. It rested there for six days prior to Moses being summoned into God's presence. As the people of Israel viewed the sight, the appearance was like a consuming fire. In Exodus 19 the scene is described in greater detail. The mountain was shrouded in smoke, which is described as looking like smoke rising from a chimney. The mountain quaked and a trumpet blast was heard at the same time. The sights and sounds must have been spectacular and awe-inspiring.

Moses later commented on this scene in Deuteronomy 5:23-24, giving further insight into the revelation of God and the response of the people. *"So it was, when you heard the voice from the midst of the darkness, while the mountain was burning with fire, that you came near to me, all the heads of your tribes and your elders. And you said: 'Surely the LORD our God has shown us His glory and His greatness, and we have heard His voice from the midst of the fire. We have seen this day that God speaks with man; yet he still lives'"* (NKJV).

The children of Israel saw the glory of God in the cloud in Exodus 16:10. The presence of the Lord was described by the word "glory." The nation of Israel was led by this cloud on their travels. The cloud is often referred to as the "Shekinah glory cloud." The word "Shekinah" does not occur in the English translation of the Bible but the Hebrew word means "the dwelling of God," or is used to depict the presence of God.

During the Israelites' journeys, the glory of God was seen in the cloud by day and the pillar of fire by night (Ex. 40:36). As they woke each morning their first sight as they exited their tents would be the cloud. It would be resting on the Tabernacle, indicating that the nation was to stay put for that

GLORY DEFINED AND DESCRIBED

day. Whenever the cloud was raised up in the sky, it was a sign that the people should pack up their tents and get ready to move. In a very real and visible way the nation of Israel was led by the glory of God.

The judgement made on those who were over 20 years old and sentenced to die in the wilderness was a result of the fact that they witnessed God's glory and His signs in Egypt yet they continued to put God to the test (Num. 14:22). Numbers 16 gives the account of the rebellion of Korah. When Korah and his followers appeared at the door of the Tabernacle with their censers, the glory of God appeared to the whole congregation. After God carried out judgement on Korah and his family, the people murmured against Moses and Aaron. Once again God's glory appeared and a deadly plague broke out in the camp. The lesson taken from these scenes is that to act in a way that defiles or depreciates God's glory is a serious matter.

IN THE TABERNACLE

God's purpose for the Tabernacle was to provide a way for Him to dwell with His people. The visible manifestation of His presence would fill the Holy of Holies. Exodus 29:43 tells us that this was possible because the Lord Himself declared, *"the tabernacle shall be sanctified by my glory."* The altar and the priests would also be sanctified to the Lord in the process. We also read that the garments of the priests and their turbans were designed for glory and beauty (Ex. 28:2, 40).

When the Tabernacle was set up in the midst of the camp and ready for service, a cloud covered the tent and *"the glory of the LORD filled the tabernacle"* (Ex. 40:34). At the start of Aaron's ministry the glory appeared as recorded in Leviticus 9. When Moses and Aaron came out of the Tabernacle, the glory was visible to all the people.

More events recorded at the start of Leviticus 10 show the gravity of diminishing God's glory. Nadab and Abihu offered strange fire before the Lord—that is, they kindled the fire in their own way contrary to God's command. They did not take the coals of the brazen altar as was required by God. God's response in judgement was to consume them with fire. God's explanation for His judgement was that these two had not regarded the holiness of God and their actions affected the glory of God (Lev. 10:3). True worship must be offered in spirit and truth with the goal of giving the glory to God.

IN THE TEMPLE

David was given the plan for the Temple by the Spirit and the Lord gave him the understanding to write down the details. David prepared a treasury of gold and silver and other material to be used on the *"house of my God"* (1 Chron. 29:3). He also referred in the same verse to the building as a "holy house."

The desire of David, and more importantly the desire of the Lord, was that the Temple would reflect the glory of God. David told Solomon that the Temple was *"not for man, but for the LORD God"* (1 Chron. 29:1). This is an important principle to carry over through the ages regarding the house of God and His dwelling place today in the church, His body.

Scripture devotes six Old Testament chapters to documenting the preparation, construction, and dedication of the Temple. This is of note when one considers that the account of creation is recorded in less than three chapters. The Temple in Jerusalem was spectacular and one of the wonders of the ancient world.

It was not just the architecture which made it splendid, *"for the glory of the LORD had filled the house of God"* (2 Chron. 5:14). 1 Kings 8 describes the filling of the Temple with the glory of God, who appeared in the form of a cloud. Solomon says of this event that, *"The LORD said He would dwell in the dark cloud"* (1 Kgs. 8:12, NKJV).

The dwelling place of God in the Temple is further described in the Psalms and the worship of Israel. The Psalmist could say, *"LORD, I have loved the habitation of Your house, And the place where Your glory dwells."* (Ps. 26:8, NKJV). The notation in the margin says the last line could be rendered literally "of the tabernacle of Your glory." Psalm 29:9 states, *"in His temple everyone says, 'Glory!'"* (NKJV).

GOD'S GLORY IN ISRAEL (THE PROSPECT)

Prophetically, glory is attached to the future appearance of Christ, relating to His person and to His reign. The Psalms declare, *"And blessed be his glorious name for ever: and let the whole earth be filled with his glory; Amen, and Amen"* (Ps. 72:19). In anticipation of Christ's reign, Psalm 96:7-8 says, *"Give unto the LORD, O ye kindreds of the people, give unto the LORD glory and strength. Give unto the LORD the glory due unto his name: bring an offering, and come into his courts."*

The city of Jerusalem will be the center of government and worship during the millennial kingdom. In the book of Zechariah it is projected to be a well-populated city and without walls. Its protection will be a wall of fire around the city; the Lord says, *"I...will be the glory in the midst of her"* (Zech. 2:5).

God will bring righteousness and salvation and place it in Zion. It is there God refers to His people as *"Israel my glory"* (Isa. 46:13). When the Lord Jesus reigns, the city will not need the sun or the moon. The Lord will be to them an everlasting light and, Isaiah says, *"your God your glory."* (Isa. 60:19, NKJV). Therefore Israel is described as God's glory and God as Israel's glory.

The prophets also speak of the Lord's future glory in relation to the millennial temple that will be built by Christ. Zechariah 6:13 states it is in this temple that He, the Messiah, will sit as the priest on His throne. He will bear the glory or, as the NIV puts it, *"he will be clothed with majesty "* (Zech. 6:13). Haggai reveals that God will fill this future temple with glory. The glory of the future temple will exceed the one of Haggai's day and *"in this place will I give peace, saith the LORD of hosts"* (Hag. 2:9).

THE GOD OF GLORY

GLORY IN THE NEW TESTAMENT (THE PRESENT)

W. E. Vine defines the New Testament use of the word "glory," as having to do with an "opinion" or "estimation." Vine says it is "the honour resulting from a good opinion." When believers give God glory they do so by expressing their estimation of His worth. "It is used of the nature and acts of God in self-manifestation, i.e., what He essentially is and does as exhibited in whatever way He reveals Himself,"[6] says Vine.

Erickson says the Greek word "conveys the meaning of brightness, splendor; magnificence and fame." God revealing His glory expresses what He is like, whether through the revelation of His grandeur, in the person of Christ, or in the whole work of redemption.

Strong's Concordance lists 11 Greek words that are translated into the word "glory" in English. As in the Old Testament, some are negative, referring to boasting or pride. Some can go either way depending on what object is in view. A positive example would be *"God forbid that I should boast except in the cross of our Lord Jesus Christ"* (Gal. 6:14, NKJV). Other positive usages mean "magnificence," "majesty," or "splendid." Some include "giving honour or praise." Ryrie gives this definition, "the glory of God is what He seems to be, which in His case is what He really is. It is God seen in some or all of His characteristics."[7]

Matthew and Luke associate glory with the birth of Christ as well as His future coming and reign. The sight the shepherds saw was glorious and they heard the words, *"Glory to God in the highest"* (Luke 2:14). In the Olivet discourse the Lord Jesus spoke of His second coming being with a display of power and glory (Matt. 24:30).

In John's gospel, glory is revealed in the person of

---

6 W. E. Vine, *An Expository Dictionary of New Testament Words* (London: Pickering and Inglis, 1939)
7 Charles C. Ryrie, *Transformed by His Glory* (Wheaton: Victor Books, 1990) 19

Christ. There John could say, *"we beheld his glory"* (John 1:14). Everything about the Lord Jesus' present position is referred to as *"his glory."* His prayer for us includes, *"Father, I desire that they also whom You gave Me may be with Me where I am, that they may behold My glory which You have given Me"* (John 17:24, NKJV).

Our salvation from start to finish is a revelation of the Lord Jesus' glory. We see the glory of His face in the gospel (2 Cor. 4:4-6) and the glory of His grace in saving us (Eph.1:6). We also witness and display His glory day-to-day as we grow in Christ (2 Cor. 3:18). There is a glory that will be ours as well when our earthly body is made like His body of glory (Phil. 3:21).

Looking to the future, the revelation of Jesus Christ will be unimaginably glorious. His reign will also be glorious. Glory will be given to Him by the nations (Rev. 21:24), and as every knee bows and every tongue proclaims Him to be Lord it will all be to the glory of God (Phil. 2: 9-11). All the angelic hosts will ascribe glory to Christ (Rev. 4:11), as will all the redeemed of this age (Rev. 5), and the redeemed of a future age (Rev. 7:12).

GIVING GOD GLORY

Believers in both testaments are called to give God glory, to declare our estimation of His person and work. *The Westminster Shorter Catechism* asks the question, "What is the chief end of man?" The answer given is, "the chief end of man is to glorify God and enjoy Him forever." To glorify God becomes an integral part of worship. It consists of expressing who He is and what He has done. Psalm 96:8-9 says that His people are to *"give unto the LORD the glory due unto his name"* and worship Him in *"the beauty of holiness."*

R. Sheldrake writes:

> God is a God of infinite variety and it is given to His own to bring glory to Him in an infinite variety of ways: some through sickness and

> death, some through life and health; some through joy and some through sorrow; some in bonds and imprisonment, some in labors more abundant; some in poverty, some in wealth, some in ill-repute, some in good repute. What matters the circumstances so long as in them we bring glory to God and in them bear testimony to God's faithfulness.

Individually or corporately, believers give Him glory as they think well or speak well of all He has done. The Lord Jesus cannot physically be given a place above the one He now has, as He has been exalted to the highest place. In our hearts however, believers can and should respond like Mary in her Magnificat, *"My soul magnifies the Lord"* (Luke 1:46, NKJV). The margin renders this phrase "My soul declares the greatness of the Lord."

To give God glory involves losing sight of self and being occupied with Him. It is lifting Him up in thought or word, in song or prayer. It involves praise, thanksgiving, and worship. As Vine stated, believers are to give God "the honour resulting from a good opinion" as we contemplate His worth.

ILLUSTRATING GLORY

Applying the important principle of "the law of first mention," we note that the word "glory" is found several times in the book of Genesis. It occurs as an **adjective** in Genesis 12:10 translated *"severe."* In verse two of the following chapter it occurs as the word *"rich."* As a **noun**, glory appears for the first time in Genesis 31:1 to describe Jacob's wealth. Here the KJV uses the word *"glory"* while the NKJV translates the word into *"wealth."* The sons of Laban are upset that their father's wealth—or glory—has been taken by Jacob. The Septuagint renders the verse, "And Jacob heard the words of the sons of Laban saying, Jacob has taken all that was our father's and of our father's property has he gotten all this glory."

GLORY DEFINED AND DESCRIBED

This reference in and of itself does not convey much significance, but when examined in the light of the second mention of glory, an interesting application is uncovered. This pattern is true of a number of biblical truths and such interconnectedness is part of what makes the study of Scripture so interesting. Consider, for example, the first two mentions of the word "love" in the Bible. The first is found in Genesis 22 describing a father's (Abraham) love for his *"only son"* (Gen. 22:2). The second mention is in Genesis 24 where the son's (Isaac) love for his bride is referenced. These two instances are representative of the story of redemption; the Father loves the Son and the Son loves the church and gave Himself for her.

Another pertinent illustration can be found in the first two occurrences of the word "worship." The word first occurs in Genesis 18 when Abraham bows before the Lord (although English translations do not necessarily make this obvious). The second mention is in Genesis 22 when Abraham says that he and Isaac will go up to the mount and worship. Thus in these two usages, worship is seen both as bowing down and as offering up.

"Glory" is found as a noun for the second time in Scripture in Genesis 45:13, describing Joseph's glory in Egypt. In these first two references to glory in the Bible we see the father's (Jacob) glory and the son's (Joseph) glory. Glory or wealth came to the father by right and the son received it by virtue of his character and conduct. The son is seen on the throne exercising dominion over the nations. His command to the brothers is to *"tell my father of all my glory in Egypt, and of all that ye have seen"* (Gen. 45:13).

The devotional thoughts which emerge from these references are rich when applied to the Father and the Son. Just as was seen in Genesis 31, the glory of this present world belongs to the Father by right. However, there exists an ongoing conflict with the children of this world wanting that glory and viewing it as their own. These thoughts can also be considered in light of the Lord Jesus' comments to the Jews in

THE GOD OF GLORY

John 8:44, *"ye are of your father the devil."* Right from the beginning Satan has coveted the glory that belonged to the Father. Isaiah 14 portrays this in the five *"I will"* statements of Satan. This is the source of the conflict of the ages.

Satan's temptation of the Lord Jesus even offered the Lord the kingdoms of the world. *"All this authority I will give You, and their glory; for this has been delivered to me, and I give it to whomever I wish"* (Luke 4:6, NKJV). Ultimately, however, the Bible declares the glory of the nations will be given to God. Revelation 21:24 says, *"the kings of the earth bring their glory to it"* (DARBY). Haggai 2:7 confirms it, *"And I will shake all nations, so that the treasures of all nations shall come in, and I will fill this house with glory, says the LORD of hosts"* (ESV). This future is also presented prophetically in Isaiah 60:1-7 through the nations bringing their wealth which will ultimately be used to glorify God's house. The last phrase of Isaiah 60:7 says, *"and I will glorify the house of my glory."* The wise men bringing wealth to the Lord Jesus were a partial fulfillment of this prophecy and also a picture of a coming day.

Satan is a defeated foe and victory at the cross assured that the Lord Jesus will indeed rule over the kingdoms of this world. Genesis 45:8-13 foreshadows the fact that the Son will be given glory and honour and His reign shall be glorious. The Suffering Servant who toiled in humility will be the exalted Sovereign and *"he shall bear the glory"* (Zech. 6:13). *"Who is this King of glory?"* (Ps. 24:10). The answer...our Lord and Saviour, Jesus Christ.

Fannie Crosby penned it well, "to God be the glory great things He hath done." The chorus ends with these words: "O come to the Father through Jesus the Son and give Him the glory—great things He hath done."

MEDITATIVE THOUGHTS

The first mention of "glory" as a noun presents a conflict between the children of this world and Jacob. The last reference to "glory" in the Old Testament is found in Malachi 2:2 with the plea of God to His priests *"to give glory unto my name."* The Lord declared, *"If ye will not hear...I will even send a curse upon you."* The last word of the Old Testament in our English translation is "curse" (Mal. 4:6).

In the New Testament, the first occurrence of "glory" is found in Matthew 4:8 where Satan showed the Lord Jesus all the kingdoms of the world and their glory. Its final mention in the Bible is in Revelation 21:24-26 where the kings of the world bring their glory and honour to Jerusalem in the eternal age.

At the end of the conflict of the ages, the glory of this world all comes to the Lord Jesus and to God the Father.

• • •

The people of Israel enjoyed an intimate association with God's glory that affected their daily life. Every morning as they exited their tents, the glory cloud was in front of them. If it was still resting on the Tabernacle, the nation did not move that day. However, if the cloud was raised up, it was time to move on. In a very tangible way the Israelites' steps and stops were directed by God's glory.

• • •

God's glory fills what belongs to Him. The visible expression of His presence occupies and then shines out. This was true in the Tabernacle the Temple, and the church and should be so in us.

• • •

There is a story in Israel's history that illustrates the importance of the presence of God in the midst of His people. It is found in the account in 1 Samuel 4 of the capture of the ark of the Lord by the Philistines. Upon hearing the news of the ark's capture, Phinehas' wife named her newborn son Ichabod which means *"the glory is departed from Israel"* (1 Sam. 4:21). This was a sad day for Israel and foreshadowed a greater departure of a future day.

It is a serious matter when God's glory departs from a local church. This could be said to be the case, however, when church life centers on "me" instead of on Him.

• • •

The following hymn, written by Joseph Addison, from the early 1700's is based on Psalm 19. In it Addison describes the unspoken revelation of God's greatness and glory.

The spacious firmament on high,
With all the blue ethereal sky,
And spangled heavens, a shining frame
Their great Original proclaim.
Th'unwearied sun, from day to day,
Does his Creator's powers display,
And publishes to every land
The work of an Almighty Hand.

Soon as the evening shades prevail
The moon takes up the wondrous tale,
And nightly to the listening earth
Repeats the story of her birth;
While all the stars that round her burn
And all the planets in their turn,
Confirm the tidings as they roll,
And spread the truth from pole to pole.

What though in solemn silence all
Move round the dark terrestrial ball?
What though no real voice nor sound
Amid the radiant orbs be found?
In reason's ear they all rejoice,
And utter forth a glorious voice,
Forever singing as they shine,
"The hand that made us is divine

CHAPTER TWO
SHOW ME YOUR GLORY

God has placed eternity in the hearts of mankind (Eccl. 3:11). Every person instinctively knows that their life lasts beyond time. It has been said that no one is born an atheist but has only come to that position through outside influence and choice. Humans have an inherent desire to know where they came from, the purpose of life, and what happens after death. The answers to these questions can only come from the One who created us. God has made Himself known through His work of creation, through His word, and through the story of redemption. God is willing to give further revelation to those who seek Him.

One way by which God reveals Himself is His glory. God's glory is the sum of His person, in **appearance, attributes,** and **activities**. The revelation of His person is glorious, bright, or dazzling in appearance. The Scripture tells us that He dwells in unapproachable light (1 Tim. 6:16). His glory is an awe-inspiring sight.

The declaration of His **character** and **conduct** is also said to be a manifestation of God's glory. Whether by visual display or verbal declaration, when God's glory is revealed mortals fall in speechless wonder.

Giving God glory in this present age is often associated with a verbal expression of praise or worship. He is given glory in song and in word. In Scripture the immediate response to God's glory was most often non-verbal, merely falling in front of Him in humility and wonder. These instances emphasize that the appropriate response to the glory of God starts in the heart and is not just a recitation of facts or a display of knowledge.

REVEALING GLORY

Since God's glory is one of the great themes of Scripture, it is fitting that all believers should cry out as Moses did, *"Please, show me Your glory"* (Ex. 33:18, NKJV). The Septuagint renders this plea, "reveal Thyself to me, that I may evidently see Thee." The translators believed that the revelation of God's glory was synonymous with a manifestation of His person.

David expressed a similar thought: *"One thing I have desired of the LORD, That will I seek: That I may dwell in the house of the LORD all the days of my life, To behold the beauty of the LORD, And to inquire in His temple"* (Ps. 27:4, NKJV). The question to ask is…"Would this be the single greatest desire in my life?"

Before Moses made his request in Exodus 33:18, he had prayed in verse 13, *"…show me now Your way, that I may know You…"* (NKJV). Moses made three requests in his conversations with God in this section of Exodus:

- He appealed for pardon (32:32).
- He asked for God's presence to go with them in Israel's travels (33:14).
- He expressed a higher and nobler desire (33:13, 18); he wanted to know more of God's person.

All believers know what it is to be **pardoned**. Some believers experience the joy of His **presence** with them day by day. Relatively few reach the level of occupation with the **person** of God as expressed in Moses' request, *"Please, show me Your glory."* This reality has been expressed another way: "In all believers Christ is **present**, in some believers Christ is **prominent** and in a few believers Christ is **pre-eminent**."

The scene around Mount Sinai in Exodus 24 illustrates well these different levels of fellowship with God. The whole congregation was gathered around the mountain. These people had just experienced redemption and deliverance by God's own hand. Out of this company Moses, Joshua, Aaron and his sons, and 70 elders enjoyed a greater fellowship with God. It was only Moses and Joshua, however, who proceeded further up the mountain and enjoyed a distinct intimacy with God.

A New Testament example is found in the crowds that surrounded the Lord Jesus. Many followed Him but, of that group, there were several women who ministered to Him and only 12 disciples. From that number just three accompanied Him up the mount of transfiguration, into Jairus' house, and further into the garden. These three saw His grace, His grief, and His glory. However, it was only John who leaned against His breast. It was only Mary who chose the better part of sitting at His feet.

There is a sense in which this level of intimacy is available to all believers. It is the road less travelled and the majority of believers do not enjoy all that is offered in Christ and of Christ. Moses, John, Mary, and countless others have gone on to the enjoyment of heaven while here on earth. On the Lord's part, He stands knocking at the door looking for individuals who desire fellowship with Him. There are some, like the two on the road to Emmaus in Luke's Gospel, who enjoyed a walk with Him. These two invited Him to come in and He obliged and ate with them. No wonder these two could speak of their heart burning within them as a result of the time spent with the Lord Jesus (Luke 24:32).

Moses' words, *"that I may know You,"* (Ex. 33:13, NKJV) are the cry of his heart. The thought is similar to what Paul expressed in Philippians 3:10, *"That I may know him."* John, in his first epistle, writes to the fathers, the spiritually mature, and commends them because they have known Him who is from the beginning (1 Jn 2:13). The challenge for today might be…what is the cry of our heart? It may be expressed in song, it maybe the desire of our heart, but is there the will to make it a reality in our life?

THE GOD OF GLORY

In response to Moses' request, God replies that no one could see God and live (Ex. 33:20). The New Testament tells us God is Spirit (John 4:24); He dwells in unapproachable light (1 Tim. 6:16); no one has seen God (John 1:18) as He is immortal and invisible (1 Tim. 1:17). God, however, does reveal Himself to mankind, His primary revelation being in the person of the Lord Jesus, the One who is the express image of His person (Heb. 1:3). God wants us to know Him and enjoy eternal intimacy with Him.

Exodus 33:21-23 describes the particulars of the revelation of God's glory. The whole scene is tied to Moses' obedience; he responded to the command of God to come up the mountain. God's glory is revealed on God's terms and not dictated by mankind.

The eternal and invisible God makes Himself known to His servant. It is while Moses was in the cleft of the rock that he was able to see the **visible** display of the radiance of God's person and presence. Moses saw the back of God, or the effect of God passing. No one can see God in all His fullness and live!

The Lord tells Moses that His goodness will pass before him. God later says, *"it shall come to pass, while my glory passeth by, that I will put thee in a clift of the rock, and will cover thee with my hand"* (Ex. 33:22). God's initial **verbal** response to Moses' request has nothing to do with God's radiance but has everything to do with His character. God speaks of His attributes and also of His activities toward man. God gives a declaration of His goodness (Ex. 33:19). The word "goodness" is often translated into English as "loving kindness."

In Exodus 34 God begins this Theophany (an appearance of God) by coming down to where Moses is standing. It is at this point that God proclaims His name (Ex. 34:5). The Psalmist speaks of the glory of God's name in Psalm 79:9, *"Help us, O God of our salvation, for the glory of thy name: and deliver us, and purge away our sins, for thy name's sake."*

God then declares His character to Moses (Ex. 34:6-7). These characteristics make the God of heaven unique, distinguishing Him from the gods invented by man: *"merciful and gracious, longsuffering, abounding in goodness and truth."* Appropriate synonyms might include compassion, grace, mercy, love, patience, and faithfulness.

God next reveals aspects of His conduct that flow from and are consistent with His character. In the Septuagint Exodus 34:7 reads, "keeping justice and mercy for thousands, taking away iniquity and unrighteousness and sins…he will not clear the guilty." The character of God is such that He is merciful and willing to forgive, yet He is consistent and therefore must also judge the guilty.

These precious attributes are the foundation of God's dealings with mankind. The gospel exudes the love, mercy, and grace of God. It also presents the righteousness of God and the wrath of God *"against all ungodliness and unrighteousness of men"* (Rom. 1:18).

The response to this experience and the revelation of God's glory is twofold in Moses' life, both God-ward and manward. In Exodus 34:8, *"Moses made haste, and bowed his head toward the earth, and worshipped."* Moses' initial reaction was one of awe and humility; he bowed and worshipped. The worship does not seem to be verbal, but rather physical; it is the very act of bowing to the earth. In this posture Moses was acknowledging the greatness of God and His right to receive worship.

This revelation of God also led Moses to make a request. The request was for God's pardon and also for His presence to go with the Israelites. In asking, Moses identified with the people, confessing that they were stiff-necked and had committed sin. He recognized that they—he and Israel—had fallen short of God's glory. We see similar God-ward reactions to the revelation of God elsewhere in Scripture.

The manward aspect of Moses' response is seen in Exodus 34:29-35. Moses' face shone with such brilliance that the Israelites were afraid to come near him. In fact Moses had to veil his face. Rabbinical tradition reports that this was true for the balance of his life. Following the experience in the cleft of the rock, it was obvious to all that Moses had been in the very presence of God, for his face reflected the glory of God.

> God does not reveal Himself hurriedly to the man on the jump. He does not unveil His heart to one who wants only a curious casual glance. He does not manifest His glory to the spiritual tourist, but to the one who comes up to Him on the Mount. The reflected glory on Moses' face as he came forth from his forty days of communion with God was not produced by a snapshot, but by a time exposure.[8]

RADIATING GLORY

The New Testament comments on this Old Testament scene in 2 Corinthians 3:7-18. The giving of the law at Mount Sinai was accompanied by a wonderful display of God's glory. This was extended to the radiance that shone from the face of Moses. In fact, this display was tied to the whole "glorious" ministry of the law.

Doctrinally this scene illustrates the superiority of this present age over the dispensation of the law. Paul explains that he is able to speak boldly or plainly about his eternal hope in Christ (2 Cor. 3:12) as opposed to the individuals in Exodus 34 for whom God's complete revelation of Himself was not yet clear. The veil that covered Moses' face was part of the lesson. The display of glory was temporary but the veil hid that fact from the children of Israel. The Jews did not see that the glory was fading, representative of the passing of the law and the greater glory associated with the Spirit's ministry in the present age. The Jewish people did not see the implications in Moses' day and, for the most part, they do not see the truth today as they are blinded to it. The veil is only removed

---

[8] A. Naismith, *1200 Notes, Quotes and Anecdotes*, (London: Pickering & Inglis, 1962). *quoted from the Choice Gleanings Calendar.

when an individual Jew turns to the Lord *"because the veil is taken away in Christ"* (2 Cor. 3:14, NKJV).

In Christ there is not only life but there is also liberty. The bondage of the law gives way to the liberty of the Spirit. With this freedom comes the privilege of seeing the glory of the Lord with an unveiled face and no diminishing of that glory.

The Scriptures are likened to a mirror. This is true in 2 Corinthians 3 and again in James 1. James speaks of the Word of God as a mirror that reveals, showing a believer what they are and what they should be. If sin is not dealt with, James says it is comparable to one who looks in a mirror and forgets what was seen.

An Old Testament mirror is found on the laver, made from the bronze looking glasses donated to the work of the Lord. The priest would come to the laver where the filth on him would be revealed, but he could be cleansed by washing in the water that flowed out of the laver. This theme is developed further in John 13 when the Lord Jesus washes the disciples' feet and pronounces them clean. The ongoing concept of cleansing is again seen in Ephesians 5 which speaks of the Lord Jesus purifying His bride with the washing of water by the word.

Here in 2 Corinthians 3:18, *"we all, with unveiled face,* [behold] *as in a mirror the glory of the Lord...being transformed into the same image from glory to glory."* It is the contemplation of God's person that leads to transformation. The word "transformed" comes from the word *metamórphōsis* in Greek, commonly used to speak of a caterpillar changing into a butterfly. For the believer there is more than the mere reflection of the image but rather a radiating from within. Christians enjoy a privilege greater than Moses in that we have Christ in us, *"the hope of glory"* (Col. 1:27).

The words by F. C. Jennings express this well and should speak to our heart.

THE GOD OF GLORY

O my Savior glorified! Now the heavens opened wide,
Show to faith's exultant eye One in beauteous majesty.

O my Savior glorified, turn my eye from all beside,
Let me but Thy beauty see—other light is dark to me.

The glory the believer can see today comes from viewing the Son of God in the Word of God. Our cleft of the rock is time spent in the Word. The Spirit of God takes the characteristics of Christ and applies them to the child of God, resulting in transformation into the image of Christ. This is a process that takes place incrementally, from one degree of glory to another (2 Cor. 3:18). When a person first trusts Christ, this glory is barely perceptible but one day will be fully revealed when we see Him.

Being focused on God's glory will transform both our worship of God and our witness to the world. Being aware of the awesomeness of God produces wonder and worship. Awe and wonder are the basis of worship and, though there is no lack of wonders, there is a serious lack of wonder. The result for today is a declining emphasis on worship.

Our testimony to the world is directly tied to our private devotional life. It is from the time spent in "the cleft of the rock," that our lives are transformed into the image of Christ. His glory may then be seen every day in our character, conversation, and conduct. As we abide in His presence we continue to "absorb His glory."

May the words of this hymn by Thomas O. Chisholm be the cry of our heart and express our desire:

I have one deep supreme desire, that I may be like Jesus
To this I fervently aspire, that I may be like Jesus
I want my heart His throne to be, so that a watching world may see
His likeness shining forth in me, I want to be like Jesus.

MEDITATIVE THOUGHTS

The cleft of the rock was a place of glory and grace—glory revealed and grace concealed. This may possibly be the same place where Elijah ended his journey and God spoke to him in a still small voice (1 Kgs. 19:12).

• • •

The revelation to Moses came out of the relationship he enjoyed with God. Communion led to greater intimacy and a grander contemplation. The journey up the mount starts with one step but the reward makes it worthwhile (see Hag. 1:7-8).

• • •

Our worship and our witness are directly tied to being alone with God. This is what Asaph realized, *"Whom have I in heaven but thee? and there is none upon earth that I desire beside thee"* (Ps. 73:25). He also states in verse 28, *"it is good for me to draw near to God: I have put my trust in the Lord God, that I may declare all thy works"*

• • •

Hebrews 2:9 says, *"we see Jesus."* Heaven is thus opened to us by the eye of faith. J. Denham Smith penned the following familiar words:

Rise my soul! Behold 'tis Jesus, Jesus fills Thy won-d'ring eyes;
See Him now in glory seated, where Thy sins no more can rise.

These are beautiful words but it has also touched my soul that the tune was supplied by Queen Victoria's husband, Albert, Prince Consort. Though nobility on earth, Albert could look up to One who died for him and now appears in heaven on his behalf.

• • •

In 2 Corinthians 3:17-18 Paul speaks of "the Lord the Spirit." According to Darby, this is the proper rendering of the phrase in verse 18. The word "Lord" is used in verse 16 of Jesus Christ and so consistency would demand the same meaning in the following two verses. This is a declaration that Christ and the Holy Spirit are One in essence though not in person. This is similar to the Lord Jesus saying *"I and my Father are one"* (John 10:30). This is also evident in the phrase *"Christ in you, the hope of glory"* (Col. 1:27). It is the Holy Spirit who seals and indwells us, yet Paul could speak of "Christ in us" because the Spirit and the Son share the same essence.

CHAPTER THREE
VISIONS OF GOD'S GLORY

There are two prophets, Isaiah and Ezekiel, who like Moses were privileged to witness a revelation of God's glory. These two were given an in-depth look into the throne room of heaven and saw God's glory. Both of these men had difficult ministries and lived in dark times. They both were tasked with proclaiming messages of judgement and doom. Despite the dark days of their time, Isaiah and Ezekiel started their respective ministries with an epiphany of glory.

Part of the encouragement would be that though times were desperate for the nation of Israel, and the Gentiles were in ascendency, God was on the throne. The prophets were assured through these visions that God does indeed rule and He gives authority to whom He will. Daniel 4:17 declares, *"the Most High rules in the kingdom of men, gives it to whomever He will, and sets over it the lowest of men"* (NKJV). King Nebuchadnezzar came to his senses when he realized that God, the Most High, is sovereign in heaven and earth and He will do as He pleases.

THE PROPHET ISAIAH

Isaiah 6 records a scene that touched Isaiah to the very core of his being. Though the vision is found six chapters into the book, this event likely took place earlier and this is but a recounting of the event. The record is likely given here because it explains Isaiah's call and commission to the work

THE GOD OF GLORY

he was to do. The scene starts with the **upward look**, followed by the **inward look,** and goes on to the **outward look**.

Isaiah's account is also notable in that the Lord Jesus refers to this occasion during His earthly ministry. *"These things Isaiah said when he saw His glory and spoke of Him"* (John 12:41, NKJV). Isaiah received a glimpse of the Lord Jesus and His pre-incarnate glory. This is the same glory Christ spoke of in His prayer, *"the glory which I had with thee before the world was"* (John 17:5).

God's glory is apprehended by all the senses in Isaiah 6. The preeminent sight is *"the LORD sitting upon a throne, high and lifted up"* (Isa. 6:1). This may have been particularly significant for Isaiah because the earthly throne had been vacated by the death of Uzziah after a 52-year reign. Yet the throne in heaven was still occupied by Adonai, the sovereign Lord. His train, or the hem of His robe, filled the temple. Because the throne is in heaven, the heavenly temple is probably in view as opposed to the Temple in Jerusalem.

Seraphs hovered above the throne. The more familiar Hebrew word *seraphim* ("im" indicates plurality and can be translated by the letter "s") indicates there were at least two of them. The word "seraphs" means "burning ones." In the singular it means "to burn." This is the same word for "fire" that was used in the sin and trespass offerings (Lev. 4:12; 5:12).[9] *"Seraph"* is also used in Numbers 21:8 to refer to the serpent on the pole (i.e. "fiery" serpent). F. C. Jennings in his *Studies in Isaiah* points out that the verse literally says, "make thee a seraph—a burning one".[10] The word "serpent" is in italics, indicating it is not in the Hebrew text but is supplied for grammatical sense in English.

The function of the seraphs is to proclaim the greatness of God and to protect the holiness of God. The covering of the face and the feet with their wings is not explained but suggests

---

9 The word for burn in the sweet savor offerings means "to convert to incense" or "to consume."
10 F. C. Jennings, *Studies in Isaiah,* (Loiseaux Bros., 1966), 67

reverence and humility. Using the other two wings to fly may speak of their readiness and willingness to respond.

Another notable facet of Isaiah's vision was the sound. The proclamation he heard was so loud and forceful that it shook the heavenly temple. The praise to the Lord moved the very foundations. Smoke filled the house, likely a result of the incense burning on the golden altar. This perfume speaks in a wonderful way of the perfections of Christ that fill the temple.

In verse 3, the threefold, awe-inspiring words *"Holy, holy, holy"* are ascribed to *"the LORD of hosts."* Few adjectives are typically used in the Hebrew language so adjectives are notably absent from the Old Testament. This fact is emphasized in comparison with the usage and abundance of adjectives in Greek and therefore in the New Testament. Instead of using adjectives, the Hebrew language shows emphasis through the use of the plural and by the repetition of words. In Isaiah 6:3, the word "holy" is repeated in order to emphasize the absolute holiness of God. Its threefold use may also be a reference to the triune nature of God which is also brought out in verse 8.

This scene is undoubtedly what R. Heber had in mind when he penned these familiar words:

> *Holy, Holy, Holy, Lord God Almighty!*
> *Early in the morning our songs shall rise to Thee;*
> *Holy, Holy, Holy! Merciful and Mighty!*
> *God in three persons, blessed Trinity!*

To this threefold declaration is added, *"the whole earth is full of his glory."* It seems that these two statements were given antiphonally, in that the one cried to the other. One seraph cried out, *"holy, holy, holy is the LORD of hosts."* The other responded, *"the whole earth is full of His glory."* This has been true all throughout history but will be manifest to all during the millennial reign of Christ.

The Psalmist reminds us that in His heavenly temple *"doth every one speak of his glory"* (Ps. 29.9). God's glory is not only the conversation of heaven, but the whole earth is full of His glory. How true are the words of Isaac Watts:

*"Lord how Thy wonders are displayed, where'er I turn my eye,
If I survey the ground I tread or gaze upon the sky."*

Another line of the same hymn says:

*"There's not a plant or flower below but makes
Thy glories known."*

The glory of God will be visible to all in a coming day. Psalm 72:19 and Habakkuk 2:14 speak of a time when all the earth will be filled with the glory of God. In that coming day the knowledge of His glory will be worldwide.

As a result of this magnificent revelation of the glory of God, Isaiah examined himself and **confessed** what he discovered. He saw his own lack of holiness and recognized the uncleanness of his lips. Isaiah declared that he had seen the King—the Lord in all His glory—and was humbled in awe (Isa. 6:5). Isaiah realized the depth of his sinfulness as he proclaimed that he was *"undone"* (or "destroyed" according to the margin reference). He recognized that he was unworthy, falling short of God's glory. Identifying with the nation of Israel, he saw himself as no better than any of his countrymen.

The Lord's gracious response was to **cleanse** Isaiah with a coal off the altar (Isa. 6:6-7). The altar referred to is likely the brazen altar because that, and not the golden altar, existed for the purpose of cleansing. The coal from the altar was symbolic of the sacrifice that was offered. The cleansing was effective because of the sacrifice.

After God's cleansing came a **call**. *"Whom shall I send, and who will go for us?"* (Isa. 6:8). The triune God issued the challenge and Isaiah responded, indicating his willingness to go.

Isaiah is given his **commission**. *"Go, and tell this people"* (Isa. 6:9). These words are often applied to the Lord Jesus but in the context here have to do with Isaiah. The task seemed straightforward, but the Lord added that the people would not listen to the message. What a difficult task, to be sent to share a message to which the people would not be responsive. The Lord looked down the years and indicated that ultimately only a tenth of the people would respond and be "for God" from out of the nation (Isa. 6:13).

The passage in Isaiah 6 uses several notable names of God. God often reveals Himself and His character through His names. In verse 8 He is referred to as *Adonai* which is translated "Lord" but has the meaning of "Master." He is the One to whom His servants respond. John 12:37-41 quotes from Isaiah, giving proof that Adonai is none other than the Lord Jesus.

The angels call Him Jehovah, which is translated *"LORD"* (Isa. 6:3) with capital letters in the KJV. This name refers to His eternal, self-existent nature, having life in Himself.

Isaiah goes on to say his eyes had seen the *"King"* (Isa. 6:5). This title is notable as well because the throne of Judah was vacant due to King Uzziah's death.

Finally God is called the *"LORD of hosts"* (Isa. 6:5), or Jehovah Sabboath. This name is primarily used by the prophets and is associated with God's dealings with His people through times of judgement. All of these titles belong to the Lord Jesus as this is a glimpse of His glory. *"The LORD of hosts, he is the King of glory"* (Ps. 24:10).

This glimpse of glory brought Isaiah to a place of confession, cleansing, calling, and commission. It touched his will as he bowed in humility and submitted to God's plan for his life. It affected his work as he performed what, at times, must have been a very discouraging ministry. Isaiah first looked upward, then he looked inward, and finally his attention was turned outward to a needy world. Certainly this is a good example for us to follow today.

THE GOD OF GLORY
THE PROPHET EZEKIEL

The book of Ezekiel contains 16 references to the glory of God. For all that is transpiring on earth in judgement there is still a sense of God's presence and purpose which transcends all in Ezekiel's writings. Early on in the book, the visible expression of God's glory is removed, but ultimately at the end of the book it is returned.

Ezekiel's first vision and his commission are laid out in the first two chapters of his book. His attention is drawn up to what is happening in the heavenlies. He saw living creatures and wheels within wheels associated with these beings. He also saw an expanse like crystal and a throne above everything else. The throne was occupied and Ezekiel describes the scene, *"As the appearance of the bow that is in the cloud in the day of rain, so was the appearance of the brightness round about. This was the appearance of the likeness of* **the glory of the Lord**" (Ezek. 1:28, emphasis added).

Ezekiel's vision began with a whirlwind coming out of the north (Ezek. 1:4). The whirlwind is described as having the appearance of fire and the colour of amber. The storm would be an ominous sign that judgement was coming on Israel out of the north.

Within this raging storm, however, Ezekiel saw evidence of God's sovereign control in the four living creatures visible within the storm. The living creatures illustrate God's intervention in the affairs of man. This scene reveals the omnipresence and the omniscience of God. He was fully aware and orchestrating this judgement. History truly is His story.

Back when I was in a youth group one of our favorite songs was this:

> *What though wars may come,*
> *With marching feet and beat of the drum,*
> *For I have Christ in my heart;*
> *What though nations rage,*

VISIONS OF GOD'S GLORY

As we approach the end of the age,
For I have Christ in my heart.
God is still on the throne, Almighty God is He;
And He cares for His own through all eternity.
So let come what may, whatever it is, I only say
That I have Christ in my heart, I have Christ in my heart
Author Unknown

Though turbulence was soon to strike Ezekiel's world, he looked up and everything above the storm spoke of stability. Habakkuk 2:20 describes this reality, *"But the LORD is in his holy temple: let all the earth keep silence before him."*

Above the living creatures, the firmament or canopy was described as *"the colour of the terrible crystal, stretched forth over their heads above"* (Ezek. 1:22). Above the canopy was the *"likeness of a throne,"* which was occupied by *"the likeness as the appearance of a man above upon it"* (Ezek. 1:26). The figure of speech Ezekiel uses is a simile (a comparison using "like" or "as"). Such comparative language is necessary because Ezekiel was describing a scene and images that are beyond our experience and comprehension.

Ezekiel's impression of the entire scene was one of brightness, and even beyond that, of brilliance. This display of the Lord's glory was spectacular in colour and appearance. The two colours were the appearance of fire and what was like *"the appearance of a rainbow in a cloud on a rainy day"* (Ezek. 1:28, NKJV).

Typically throughout Scripture fire speaks of God's justice and holiness. This was the prominent feature of the impending storm. Ezekiel sees the One of whom it could be said, *"For our God is a consuming fire"* (Heb. 12:29). This is reminiscent of the burning holiness of God. However, the fire was accompanied by the appearance of a rainbow which we know to be God's divinely appointed sign of grace (Gen. 9:16). Ezekiel's vision portrays a throne of **government,** but it is also a throne of **grace**.

THE GOD OF GLORY

Ezekiel glimpsed several other views of God's glory according to Scripture. One such instance took place on a wide level plain, *"the glory of the LORD stood there, as the glory which I saw by the river of Chebar"* (Ezek. 3:23). Another happened when he was in his own house. He saw a variation of his vision in chapter one. This time there was no reference to the rainbow and therefore the accompanying suggestion of grace. He could report, *"behold, the glory of the God of Israel was there, according to the vision that I saw in the plain"* (Ezek. 8:4).

In Ezekiel 3:12 there is a movement of the Spirit of God and God announces, *"Blessed be the glory of the LORD from his place"* (Ezek. 3:12). Sadly, this is exactly what Israel did not do—give God His glory in the temple.

In chapters 10 and 11, Ezekiel saw the glory of the Lord in association with the Temple and the city of Jerusalem. The glory is seen leaving the Temple, and then at the east gate of the Temple. Finally it is seen on the mountain on the east side of the city, the Mount of Olives. This is the route David took when he fled the city during the rebellion of Absalom. This is a journey that also foreshadowed that of the Lord Jesus as He left the Temple, the city, and finally ascended from the same place on the Mount of Olives.

Ezekiel did not see that glory again until much later in the book when he wrote, *"the glory of the God of Israel came from the way of the east"* (Ezek. 43:2). He goes on to say, *"the glory of the LORD came into the house by the way of the gate whose prospect is toward the east. So the spirit took me up, and brought me into the inner court; and, behold, the glory of the LORD filled the house"* (Ezek. 43:4-5). This passage anticipates the return of the Lord Jesus to the Mount of Olives, His entrance into the city, and finally His arrival at the Temple.

The theme of God's glory permeates the book of Ezekiel and bookends all that transpires. The last words of Ezekiel's prophecy are Jehovah Shammah, *"The LORD is there"* (Ezek. 48:35). The glory of God will reside in Jerusalem again throughout the millennium.

It is these recorded displays of God's glory that allow Ezekiel, and us who read, to make sense of all the judgements that are uttered in this book. The events are not arbitrary but under God's control and purposed to bring Him glory. Ezekiel could have said, "I do not know what the future holds but I know who holds the future." As the words of this hymn by Ira Stanphill remind us, he could continue on because the Lord is on the throne:

Many things about tomorrow, I don't seem to understand,
But I know Who holds tomorrow, And I know Who holds my hand

Ezekiel's response to the visions in 1:28 and in 3:23 was to fall on his face. His posture reveals humility and worship. As a precursor to his difficult commission, he received a glimpse of the government and glory of God. His response was worship! From that posture, the Spirit of God picked him up and gave him a mission. Worship once again precedes work and witness for the Lord. This vision of glory would strengthen and sustain Ezekiel in a very trying ministry.

For both Isaiah and Ezekiel, the content of their message was one of judgement on their own people. They exposed their wickedness and God's wrath. Both needed to know that God's actions were not arbitrary but that God was on the throne and His purposes would come to fruition.

MEDITATIVE THOUGHTS

A glimpse of God's glory should precede our work for God. The upward look is the preparation for the outward look. Worship must be the starting point in order for our service for the Lord to be effective.

• • •

Isaiah and Ezekiel teach us that a revelation of God's glory is key to His people being able to persevere despite impossible tasks and difficult circumstances.

• • •

Psalm 99 is organized in three sections. Each section contains the phrase *"is holy"* (Ps. 99: 3, 5, 9) in reference to God—another example of threefold emphasis on God's holiness. Interestingly, the Lord is also presented as Prophet, King, and Priest throughout the psalm.

• • •

"May the glory of the LORD be praised in his [dwelling] *place"* (Ezek. 3:12, NLT). The dwelling of the Lord today is in the church, the temple of the living God. So often people approach church life asking, "what is in it for me?" or "what can I get out of it?" Our first priority should be, "how can I serve and function for God's glory?"

• • •

In response to the proclamation of the seraphs, the posts of the doors were shaken (Isa. 6:4). Jennings renders this phrase, "And the foundations of the threshold shook at the voice of them that cried." If inanimate objects were moved by God's glory, how much more should His own people be awed by His holiness and glory.

• • •

Immortal, invisible, God only wise,
In light inaccessible hid from our eyes,
Most blessèd, most glorious, the Ancient of Days,
Almighty, victorious, Thy great Name we praise.

Unresting, unhasting, and silent as light,
Nor wanting, nor wasting, Thou rulest in might;
Thy justice, like mountains, high soaring above
Thy clouds, which are fountains of goodness and love.

To all, life Thou givest, to both great and small;
In all life Thou livest, the true life of all;
We blossom and flourish as leaves on the tree,
And wither and perish—but naught changeth Thee.

Great Father of glory, pure Father of light,
Thine angels adore Thee, all veiling their sight;
But of all Thy rich graces this grace, Lord, impart
Take the veil from our faces, the vile from our heart.

All laud we would render; O help us to see
'Tis only the splendor of light hideth Thee,
And so let Thy glory, Almighty, impart,
Through Christ in His story, Thy Christ to the heart.

Walter Chalmers Smith

CHAPTER FOUR

WE BEHELD HIS GLORY

An Old Testament revelation of God is referred to as a Theophany (an appearance of God), or a Christophany (a pre-incarnate appearance of Christ). Isaiah's vision in chapter 6 of his book is referred to by the Lord Jesus as an appearance of Himself in His pre-incarnate glory. This revelation to Isaiah took place in **time** but the Lord Jesus also mentioned the glory He had before the foundation of the world, in **eternity** (John 17:5).

The glory of the pre-incarnate Christ which was revealed to Isaiah (Isa. 6) and to Ezekiel (Ezek. 1) was veiled while the Lord Jesus was on earth. Philippians 2 describes the steps of the Lord Jesus from heaven to earth, from visible glory to veiled glory. Christ is the very form or essence of God so He did not think that the visible expression of equality was something to grasp after. The eternal reality of this equality with God would not, nor could not, change, even if the outward and visible presentation should be altered.

The Lord Jesus voluntarily humbled Himself. The visible expression of His inward reality was that of a servant. Scripture tells us that Christ humbled Himself, *"being found in appearance as a man"* (Phil. 2:8, NKJV). His servanthood was further demonstrated by His perfect obedience *"to the point of death, even the death of the cross"* (Phil. 2:8, NKJV). In order to take on humanity, Christ had to veil His resplendent glory, that is, the visible display of glory or brightness. He never ceased to be what He always was (fully God), yet He became what He had never been (fully man).

Philippians 2:7 uses the Greek word *kenosis* in the phrase *"made Himself of no reputation"* (NKJV). The ESV renders this phrase *"emptied Himself."* The Lord Jesus voluntarily left His glory. As J. B. Lightfoot put it in his commentary on Philippians, He divested Himself of the insignia of majesty.[11] Philippians 2 gives other examples of those who divested themselves of their rights. Paul, Timothy, and Epaphroditus all emptied themselves in the service of others. These three exhibited the mind of, or the same attitude as, the Lord Jesus.

The incarnate Christ was able to, and did indeed, display His glory while here on earth. His resplendent glory was veiled, but His **inherent** (i.e. permanent or characteristic) and **intrinsic** (i.e. natural or essential) glory still shone. The glory which cannot be separated from His character, conduct, and conquest was readily seen.

THE GLORY OF HIS PERSON

In the synoptic gospels (Matthew, Mark, and Luke) glory is associated with the birth of Christ and with His future appearance. The whole of His earthly life is bookended with glory. In Luke 2:9 the angels who appeared to the shepherds were accompanied by a visible display of God's glory that shone around them. The angelic announcement included the words, *"Glory to God in the highest"* (2:14).

In Matthew 16:27, the Lord Jesus prophesied of His future return to earth when He would come in the glory of His Father. Matthew 24:30 describes His second coming as being in *"power and great glory."*

John's gospel takes us to the end of Christ's earthly life. The Lord's prayer in John 17 shows the reader His request for the manifestation of His pre-incarnate glory. Very soon, the name of the Father would be glorified in and through the

---
11 J. B. Lightfoot, *Philippians*, (Wheaton: Crossway Books), 1994

death of the Son (John 12:28). A further word of testimony in the epistles is found in 1 Timothy 3:16 where we read He was *"received up in glory."*

The focus of John's gospel is to present the Lord Jesus as the Son of God. His deity is affirmed and acclaimed. The eternal Word was made flesh; He dwelt among men as the incarnate Word and was seen in all His inherent glory (John 1:14). Glimpses are given of His past, present, and prospective glory. These aspects are associated with the **person**, **power**, **passion,** and present **position** of the Lord Jesus. As if viewing a diamond from different angles, John records various aspects of the Lord Jesus' glory.

John wrote in John 1:14 that he and others saw a display of glory when viewing the Lord Jesus, *"we beheld his glory."* This could be a reference to the transfiguration and the radiance seen on that occasion. In the context it seems more likely that the reference is to His person and character which is described as *"full of grace and truth."*

John 1:18 states that the Son, who resides in the Father's bosom, *"declared"* the invisible God during His time on earth. This same thought is expressed in Hebrews 1:1-4 where we read, *"God...has in these last days spoken to us by His Son"* (NKJV). God has revealed Himself *"in His Son,"* or more literally "in Son." The word "His" is in italics, indicating it is not present in the Greek text and the translators included the pronoun in order for the sentence to make sense in English. The profound significance of the text is that the Son is more than a messenger (like the prophets), He **is** the message. He is *"the brightness of his glory, and the express image of his person"* (Heb. 1:3). All of God's fullness was at home in the Lord Jesus in bodily form (Col. 1:19; 2:9).

John's account of the incarnation is summed up in John 1:14, *"the Word was made flesh."* The Lord Jesus *"dwelt among us"* (NKJV) or "tabernacled" with man. Just as in the Old Testament Tabernacle, God's glory was resident in Christ. John could say that the glory of the only begotten of the Father was made visible. The words *"only begotten"* do not refer to "generation" or "birth" but to the priority of Christ's person. This is why some Bible versions render the phrase as *"the one and only"* (NIV) both here and in John 3:16.

The manifestation of God's glory was in His person which J.G. Bellet called—in a classic book on the topic—*The Moral Glories of Christ*. This glory shone in all that He did and was and was a display that could not be hidden. So John could say, *"...and we beheld his glory, the glory as of the only begotten of the Father, full of grace and truth"* (John 1:14).

The Lord Jesus is the embodiment of **grace**. In the Gospels, grace is associated with the person of Christ; it speaks of His character. According to Titus 2:11, grace was revealed on earth in the person of Christ, *"for the grace of God that bringeth salvation hath appeared to all men."* His lips were full of grace so that His speech was gracious. He overflowed or abounded with grace, super-abounding grace (John 1:16).

It was this display of grace touching so many lives that led the crowd to say, *"He hath done all things well"* (Mark 7:37). Peter said of Him, *"neither was guile* [deceit] *found in his mouth"* (1 Pet. 2:22). It is amazing to think that the Lord Jesus never had to retract a word or apologize for saying the wrong thing. His speech was always seasoned with grace (Col. 4:6).

The Lord Jesus was also **truth** in the flesh. As the eternal Word (that is, God manifest in the flesh) He could say, *"I am... the truth"* (John 14:6). God's word is truth (John 17:17), the Holy Spirit is the Spirit of truth (John 16:13), and the Lord Jesus is truth. Truth by its very nature is absolute and exclusive. The Lord's character, conduct, and conversation were the living representation of truthfulness. The glory of His person in grace and truth was in full display while He walked on earth.

THE GLORY OF HIS POWER

According to John 2:11, the Lord Jesus' works or power also *"manifested forth his glory"* (the NLT translates "manifested" as *"revealed"*). This passage refers to the first of a series of seven signs performed by Christ in the Gospel of John before His death on the cross. The sign referred to in John 2:11, of changing water into wine, demonstrated His transformational power—that is, His ability to replace emptiness with joy. The six water pots He used were intended for Jewish ceremonial washing, an outward and ritualistic manifestation of righteousness. These jars were empty, much like the Jewish religion had become, devoid of inward reality. The Lord Jesus performed an inner, unseen work that transformed water into wine.

There are encounters with six individuals in John's Gospel that in a devotional way could be represented by these empty pots. All six discovered that their spiritual life was empty, lacking reality and joy. These encounters can be grouped in three couplets.

Nicodemus (John 3) and the Samaritan woman (John 4) both found that the Lord Jesus had the answers to the longing of their souls. Though these two were opposites in many ways (for example, male versus female, Jew versus Gentile), both were steeped in religious practice. They were seeking for something that would satisfy. The Lord Jesus presented them with the truth of eternal life based on a relationship and not religion.

The second grouping contains the nobleman's son (John 4:46-53) and the man with the infirmity by the pool of Bethesda (John 5:1-15). The nobleman's son as well as the infirm man both faced hopeless situations that their religious beliefs could not remedy. Their lives changed irrevocably when they met the Lord Jesus.

Thirdly, both the blind man of John 9 and Lazarus in John 11 were in need, beyond hope, and past help. The blind man received sight and Lazarus was brought back to life. In John 9 the disciples asked who had sinned to cause the man's blindness, the man or his parents. The Lord responded that the situation had happened so that God's power might be seen. In the case of Lazarus, the situation was *"for the glory of God, that the Son of God might be glorified thereby"* (John 11:4). In all of these lives the transforming work of the Lord was unseen, from the inside out. Wholeness, satisfaction, and joy were the results. It is the Lord's power that transformed these lives. He gave new life, brought wholeness, and restored what was lost.

The servants' only part in the miracle in John 2 was to obey what the Lord Jesus told them to do. Mary's words in John 2:5 are the only command given by her recorded in Scripture. Good advice for every believer down through the ages, Mary said, *"Whatsoever he saith unto you, do it."*

The servants filled the water pots, but they had no power to perform the inner transformation. So it is today. Believers share the gospel, pouring it into empty vessels by the preaching of the word. The inner unseen work is done by the Lord and is to His glory. Every soul that is saved is a miracle of grace through faith, so no one could boast, all to the glory of God (Eph. 2:8-9).

THE GLORY OF HIS PASSION

The glory of Christ's passion is introduced in John 12:27 and seen again in 13:31-32. In response to the request of the Greeks to see Jesus, the Lord said, *"The hour is come, that the Son of man should be glorified"* (John 12:23). Up to this point in His ministry the Lord Jesus had said, *"My time is not yet come"* (John 7:6), or *"my time is not yet full come"* (John 7:8).

In John 12:28 the Lord prayed for the Father to glorify His name. The response from heaven came, *"I have both glorified it, and will glorify it again."* The cross is in view in John 12 as the Lord Jesus spoke of a grain of wheat falling into the ground and dying. In John 13:31-32 it is the cross as well as the resurrection and ascension that are referenced. The Lord's prayer makes a similar request regarding the Father's glory, *"Father, the hour is come; glorify thy Son, that thy Son also may glorify thee"* (John 17:1).

The great glory of the cross, first and foremost, is that the Father's will was accomplished. This is what is foreshadowed in the burnt offering of Leviticus 1. A voluntary worship offering was to be given out of love and devotion as a sweet savour to God.

Beyond that, God's glory shines through many of the attributes which were displayed at the cross. Mercy and truth met together, and righteousness and peace kissed each other (Ps. 85:10). The love of the Father is fully seen at the cross in that He gave His only Son as a sacrifice for us. This is how John describes love in his epistle, that God loved us and gave His Son as a sacrifice for us (1 Jn. 4:10).

The passion of the cross also glorifies the Lord Jesus—in redemption and in renown. At the cross Christ took the place of the sacrificial Lamb, the substitutionary offering, and the Good Shepherd who died for the sake of the flock. At the cross He defeated Satan's power over death and freed us from the bondage of fear. The Lord Jesus also satisfied the just demands of a holy God and paid the price for our sins (Rom. 6:23).

The Father glorified the Son through His work on the cross and, ever since, His people have given Him glory for His great love for us and the redemption found in Him. This is displayed visibly whenever the Lord's people meet to observe the Lord's Supper. *"For as often as you eat this bread and drink this cup, you proclaim the Lord's death till He comes "* (1 Cor. 11:26). What starts here and now will continue through all of eternity; worship and glory will be given to the Lamb who was slain.

Thomas Kelly's lovely words are a fitting summary of the work of the Lord Jesus on the cross.

Glory, glory everlasting be to Him who bore the cross,
Who redeemed our souls by tasting death, the death deserved by us.
Spread His glory, Who redeemed His people thus!

His is love, 'tis love unbounded, without measure, without end;
Human thought is here confounded, 'Tis too vast to comprehend.
Praise the Savior! Magnify the sinner's Friend!

THE GOD OF GLORY

While we tell the wondrous story of the Savior's cross and shame,
Sing we, Everlasting glory be to God and to the Lamb.
Hallelujah! Give ye glory to His Name!

THE GLORY OF HIS POSITION

John chapter 17 contains another request by the Lord Jesus with respect to the glory of the cross. The request, outlined in verse 5, has to do with the restoration of His former glory in view of His finished work on earth. This reference is made to the positional glory of the Lord Jesus. Christ now occupies an exalted place, *"seated...at* [the Father's] *right hand in the heavenly places, far above all principality and power and might and dominion, and every name that is named, not only in this age but also in that which is to come"* (Eph. 1:20-21, NKJV).

The New Testament gives us several brief glimpses of Christ's restored glory following His ascension. Stephen's well known discourse in Acts 7:2 begins with a reference to the God of glory taken from the life of Abraham. Acts 7:55 tells us that Stephen, *"being full of the Holy Spirit, gazed into heaven and saw the glory of God, and Jesus standing at the right hand of God"* (NKJV). The discourse ends with an exclamation, *"Look! I see the heavens opened and the Son of Man standing at the right hand of God!"* (Acts 7:56, NKJV).

Paul was arrested on the road to Damascus in Acts 9 by the glory of the risen Christ. The display of light was both brilliant and blinding to Paul. Each time the story of his conversion is retold, the light is described as being brighter. In Acts 22:6 it is *"a great light from heaven"* (NKJV). Before Agrippa in Acts 26:13 Paul said, *"I saw a light from heaven, brighter than the sun."* As a result of this display of God's glory, Paul acknowledged the sovereignty of the Lord Jesus, twice calling Him *"Lord"* (Acts 9:5, 6). The second time is in the form of a question, *"Lord, what do You want me to do?"* (NKJV).

The Lord Jesus is now at the right hand of the Majesty on high. He is over all things, Head of the church (Eph. 5:23), and He has a more excellent name than the angels (Heb. 1:4), a name which is above every name (Eph. 1:21). He is the Great High Priest (Heb. 4:14), He is the Chief Shepherd (1 Pet. 5:4), and He is the heavenly Bridegroom.

A good illustration of the acquired glories of Christ can be found in David's life with respect to his conquest of Goliath. 1 Samuel 17:25 lists the three rewards that would be given to one who could kill the giant. The victor would be enriched with great riches, the king's daughter would become his wife, and his family would be free of taxes. David conquered the giant and, in time, all of these rewards were granted him. He took the enemy's sword and armor to his own tent and made a show of his triumph openly. He was praised by the people and exalted to the head of the army by Saul. The nation was freed from the bondage of the fear of death. David ultimately went from being a shepherd to a sovereign, from obscurity to renown, and from rejection to reigning.

As great as these honours were, they pale in comparison to what the Lord Jesus, David's greater Son, gained by His victory. The Lord Jesus has been *"crowned with glory and honor"* (Heb. 2:9), a bride is being gathered for Him, and all who have a relationship with Him by faith are free in Him. Christ is the very One who tasted death for every man and is now exalted to the highest place.

A.P. Gibbs rendered it this way:

> *But now He's risen ascended crowned,*
> *On the throne! On the throne.*
> *Heaven's highest place for Him is found,*
> *On the throne! On the throne.*
> *Our hearts we low in worship bow, and join,*
> *as one to hail Him now:*
> *"Worthy O Lamb of God art Thou!"*
> *On the throne! On the throne.*

MEDITATIVE THOUGHTS

The symbolism of Christ washing His disciples' feet in John 13 is a wonderful picture of the stoop the Lord Jesus took from heaven to earth. In verse 4 He rose and laid aside His garments. Then He took a towel and wrapped Himself with it—the garb of a servant. The Lord Jesus proceeded to do the work of a servant in that He washed the feet of the disciples. Verse 12 says He took up His garments and sat down again. What a simple illustration of the actions taken by the Lord Jesus in Philippians 2:5-11.

• • •

The garments of Joseph in Genesis are significant. The coat of many colours was given to the **beloved son** of Jacob. Joseph left his robe in the hand of Potiphar's wife as he fled; this was the garment of a **slave**. When he was released from prison, his prison clothes were removed; these were the garments of one who **suffered**. Finally Joseph was given royal robes by Pharaoh, the regal robes of a **sovereign**. Joseph's life story is another illustration of the path Christ took as described in Philippians 2:5-11.

• • •

In the Gospel of John, various aspects of the Lord's glory are presented: His pre-incarnate glory; His moral glory; the glory of His work; the glory of the cross; His acquired glory; and His positional glory.

• • •

A. P. Gibbs was an accomplished hymn writer who wrote "Worthy, Incarnate Word, to be Adored," and

"We Would Remember Thee." He also added final verses to four hymns found in *Hymns of Worship and Remembrance*. Three of these hymns originally ended with a view of Christ on the cross. Gibbs wrote final verses that present Christ as glorified and seated above with the Father. The hymns are: "Behold, Behold the Lamb of God," "Down from the Throne Eternal," and "Nailed upon Golgotha's Tree."

Throned in glorious majesty, Lord triumphant—Who is He?
E'en the same Who came to die, now in heav'n, exalted high
With adoring hearts we now at His blessed feet would bow.
Lord of all, 'tis He, 'tis He, throned in glorious majesty.

Thomas Kelly was put out of the established church for preaching the whole counsel of God. He served in Dublin in the 1840's during a time of famine. He wrote many hymns including "Praise the Savior Ye Who Know Him" and the following:

Glory to God on high, Peace upon earth and joy,
Goodwill to man! We who God's blessing prove,
His name all names above, Sing now the Savior's love
Too vast to scan.

Mercy and truth unite, Oh, 'tis a wondrous sight,
All sights above! Jesus the curse sustains,
Guilt's bitter cup He drains, Nothing for us remains,
Nothing but love.

Love that no tongue can teach, Love that no thought can reach,
No love like His! God is its blessed source,
Death ne'er can stop its course, Nothing can stay its force,
Matchless it is.

Blest in this love we sing, to God our praises bring,
All sins forgiven: Jesus, our Lord, to Thee
Honor and majesty Now and forever be
Here, and in heaven.

CHAPTER FIVE

THE GLORY OF HIS GRACE

The salvation of mankind was described in a wonderful sermon given by evangelist E. V. Hill at Moody called "God at His Best." This message can still be accessed online (though he is dead, he yet speaks). In his sermon, Hill described redemption as a greater work than the creation of the universe, greater than the flood, the exodus, or the miracles of Christ on earth. He ended the message with these words, "When He saved my soul, cleansed and made me whole, it took a miracle of love and grace." That was his bottom line—God at His best, showing mercy to sinners.

The salvation now revealed through the work of Christ is so amazing that the Old Testament writers wished to know more about it. The Old Testament prophets wrote about grace being given to the Gentiles and the sufferings and subsequent glories of Christ, but they did not know the particulars (1 Pet. 1:10-11). Scripture tells us that the angels of heaven desire to look into and understand those things believers enjoy (1 Pet. 1:12).

The following words were written in the 1700's by Samuel Davies who was the second president of Princeton University. The original words were different than the more familiar ones now sung in *Hymns of Worship and Remembrance*. The hymn is based on Micah 7:18, *"Who is a God like You, Pardoning iniquity And passing over the transgression of the remnant of His heritage? He does not retain His anger forever, Because He delights in mercy"*

(NKJV). Micah goes on to say in verse 19, *"You will cast all our sins Into the depths of the sea"* (NKJV).

> *Great God of wonders! All thy ways*
> *Display thine attributes divine;*
> *But countless acts of pardoning grace*
> *Beyond thine other wonders shine:*
> *Who is a pardoning God like thee?*
> *Or who has grace so rich and free?*
>
> *Crimes of such horror to forgive,*
> *Such guilty, daring worms to spare;*
> *This is thy grand prerogative,*
> *And none may in this honor share:*
> *Who is a pardoning God like thee?*
> *Or who has grace so rich and free?*
>
> *In wonder lost, with trembling joy*
> *We take the pardon of our God;*
> *Pardon for crimes of deepest dye,*
> *A pardon bought with Jesu's blood:*
> *Who is a pardoning God like thee?*
> *Or who has grace so rich and free?*
>
> *O may this strange, this matchless grace,*
> *This God-like miracle of love,*
> *Fill the wide earth with grateful praise,*
> *As now it fills the choirs above!*
> *Who is a pardoning God like thee?*
> *Or who has grace so rich and free?*

Ephesians 1:3-14 describes the wonder of God's redemptive work and three times over proclaims that it was all for His glory (vv. 6, 12, 14). Salvation from start to finish is all about what God has done; the only part that belongs to man is to hear the gospel and to trust or believe (Eph. 1:13). Verses 3 to 14 speak of the work of the Father, the Son, and the Holy Spirit. Though various English translations punctuate this passage differently, it could be left as one complete sentence (as in the KJV).

THE GLORY OF HIS GRACE

GOD'S GLORY AND OUR SALVATION

Ephesians 1:3-6 states that the Father's purposes for us are fulfilled in Christ and that all blessings come to us in Christ. These blessings include the fact that all believers are made holy and blameless and enjoy adoption as sons. This work of the Father, making believers *"accepted in the beloved"* was a work that was all to *"the praise of the glory of his grace."*

In verses 7 to 12 it is the person of the Lord Jesus Christ that is in view. His work in redemption, revelation, and the reconciliation of all things is presented. Paul in particular refers to Jews of the first century who were saved. Note the different pronouns that are used: *"us"* through most of the passage; *"we"* in verses 11 and 12; *"you"* in verse 13; and *"our"* in 14. The *"we"* in verses 11 and 12 refers to Jews saved in the first century. Paul concludes that these converts are *"to the praise of his glory, who first trusted in Christ."*

In Ephesians 1:13-14, Scripture reveals that the presence of the Holy Spirit in us is a seal for our security. It is the fulfillment of the promise of the Lord Jesus. The phrase in verse 13 may be rendered *"the Holy Spirit of promise"* (NKJV). This distinct work of the Holy Spirit is also said to be to *"the praise of His glory"* (NKJV).

Paul's treatise on the great work of salvation in Ephesians 1 displays the wonder of God's grace. It is *"according to the riches of his grace"* (v. 7) that God has redeemed us and extended to us the forgiveness of sins. His grace allows believers to be accepted in the beloved. God receives glory because of His amazing grace.

Paul explains in Ephesians 2:8 that salvation is a gift from God received by faith. The gender of the various words in the Greek text, not evident in the English translation, makes it more logical that salvation is the gift which is referred to and it is received by faith. Faith is not a work but merely the acceptance of what God offers as a free gift. The fact that salvation is from God and not of works eliminates the possibility of human effort, thus removing any ground for boasting. All the glory of salvation goes to God as believers are His workmanship and recipients of His gift.

MY TRIBUTE

How can I say thanks
For the things You have done for me,
Things so undeserved,
Yet You gave to prove Your love for me.
The voices of a million angels
Could not express my gratitude.
All that I am and ever hope to be,
I owe it all to Thee.

Chorus
To God be the glory,
To God be the glory,
To God be the glory,
For the things He has done.
With His blood He has saved me,
With His power He has raised me,
To God be the glory,
For the things He has done.

Just let me live my life,
Let it be pleasing, Lord, to Thee,
And if I gain any praise,
Let it go to Calvary.
With His blood He has saved me,
With His power He has raised me,
To God be the glory,
For the things He has done.

Words and Music by Andrae Crouch
© 1971 Bud John Songs, Inc.

The principle of salvation being completely of God is also found in 1 Corinthians 1. Here the gospel is called *"foolishness"*

THE GLORY OF HIS GRACE

by the unsaved (1 Cor. 1:23) yet it is God's means to reach the perishing. The type of people God reaches and saves are often held in low esteem by the world (1 Cor. 1:26-27). God purposely uses what is despised by man, what is of no account, so that it becomes obvious that the work is of God. This way no one could possibly take credit for or even share in the glory of what God does.

1 Corinthians 1 contains Paul's elaboration on what believers have in and through Christ. Christ has become for us *"righteousness, and sanctification, and redemption"* (v. 30). The wisdom of God is displayed in all that Christ is to us. Christ is our source of righteousness, He is the cause of our sanctification, and He is the certainty for the redemption of our bodies. All of these truths are for the glory of the Lord and they assure that all glory for the work of salvation goes to Him (1 Cor. 1:29-31).

Paul referred to the message he preached as *"the glorious gospel of Christ,"* adding this description, *"who is the image of God"* (2 Cor. 4:4). Satan blinds the minds of unbelievers lest the light of Christ's glory should shine on them and they should be converted. For believers, it is only because this light shone in our hearts that we received *"the light of the knowledge of the glory of God in the face of Jesus Christ"* (2 Cor. 4:6).

Romans tells us that the gospel is *"the power of God unto salvation"* (Rom. 1:16). Paul recognized that the privilege of preaching the gospel was a matter of God's grace and that it was God who gave the increase (1 Cor. 3:7). The fruit of Paul's preaching was a result of the Word of God sprouting as an incorruptible seed in a person's life. Spiritual life comes from above, given by the Holy Spirit. All of these scriptural truths demonstrate that salvation is of the Lord and leaves man no room to boast.

Paul claimed that on a human level, both with respect to his pedigree and in his person, he had much about which to boast in an earthly sense, but he counted it all as loss. He declared that the only boast he would make was in the cross of our Lord Jesus Christ (Gal. 6:14). In various places in the New Testament, Paul stated that his motive—in eating and drinking, in the presenting of the gospel, even his view on financial support—was bringing glory to God.

Salvation involves more than being saved from the penalty of sin. As wonderful as that fact is, it is but a part of our salvation. The sanctification of the believer has past, present, and prospective implications, all of which express the glory of God.

GOD'S GLORY AND OUR SANCTIFICATION

Positional sanctification is a result of the act of justification where the believer is given the righteousness of Christ. As we have seen previously, our standing is all of God, not of works, and thus to His glory and praise.

Progressive sanctification relates to the believer's state, that is, practical holiness day by day. This type of santification occurs over time and is a result of several factors. On the believer's side it has to do with purity, obedience, fellowship, and separation. On the divine side it has to do with God's work in us. The Holy Spirit progressively changes us into the image of Christ, from one degree of glory to another. God leads us to maturity so that we desire to do His will, *"working in you that which is wellpleasing in his sight, through Jesus Christ; to whom be glory for ever and ever"* (Heb. 13:20-21).

Perfect sanctification is the future prospect for every believer—to be like the person of the Lord Jesus. Scripture tells us that our earthly bodies will be *"conformed to His glorious body"* (Phil. 3:21, NKJV). Jude says it is God who is able to keep us and present us *"faultless before the presence of his glory with exceeding joy"* (Jude 24). Jude 25 goes on to say, *"To the only wise God our Saviour, be glory and majesty, dominion and power, both now and ever. Amen."*

THE GLORY OF HIS GRACE

GOD'S GLORY AND OUR SUFFERING

Romans 5:2 explains that believers have come into God's grace and, as a result, *"rejoice in hope of the glory of God."* All believers were at one time sinners who fell short of the glory that is now such a source of joy. Grace makes hope not only possible but a reality. Every believer has Christ in them as the hope of, or certainty of, the glory that is to follow (Col. 1:27).

Beyond that, Paul's next words run counter to our human experience. *"And not only so, but we glory in tribulations"* (Rom. 5:3). James tells us to consider it all joy when we fall into various trials. The word *"count"* used in James 1:2 is an accounting word that carries the idea of "consider it an asset." Peter uses different wording, but he also tells believers to greatly rejoice in the midst of various trials (1 Pet. 1:6). The reason for joy in such times is that tribulation and trials produce a result. Experiences and circumstances are used by God to develop character and to prove our faith. Peter's epistle says that genuine faith is of greater value than gold that will perish. Faith that has been tested will bring glory to God at the appearing of Jesus Christ (1 Pet. 1:7).

Suffering for the sake of Christ is what believers are to expect. The Lord Himself spoke of the world's hatred of Him and His followers. Philippians 1:29 says it has been granted to us not only to believe in Christ but also to suffer for His sake. Peter puts it this way, *"Beloved, do not think it strange concerning the fiery trial which is to try you, as though some strange thing happened to you; but rejoice to the extent that you partake of Christ's sufferings, that when His glory is revealed, you may also be glad with exceeding joy. If you are reproached for the name of Christ, blessed are you, for the Spirit of glory and of God rests upon you"* (1 Pet. 4:12-14, NKJV).

Many believers over the centuries have suffered graciously and even died courageously to the glory of God. It is in times of difficulty that believers find refuge in the *"God of all comfort"* (2 Cor. 1:3). They find that God's grace is sufficient, and that

THE GOD OF GLORY

His strength is made perfect in weakness (2 Cor. 12:9). As a result of these divine resources, many have praised God even in the midst of sorrow. The experience of Job rings true, *"The LORD gave, and the LORD has taken away; Blessed be the name of the LORD"* (Job 1:21, NKJV). Job made this declaration while he was prostrate on the ground worshipping God.

GOD'S GLORY AND OUR SUFFICIENCY

Providence and the provisions that believers enjoy come from the hand of God, *"according to his riches in glory by Christ Jesus"* (Phil. 4:19). There is nothing that one can boast about as if it came from us. This is true in the temporal realm as God supplies all our needs as every good and perfect gift comes from Him (Jas. 1:17). It is true in the spiritual realm as well because His grace is **sufficient** for us. We are **strengthened** by grace, we **stand** in it, and we **serve** because of it. Our salvation, standing, security, and sanctification are all to the glory of God. Our service, supplication, and suffering are also to His glory. These things are true in time and will continue to be so throughout the endless ages.

When Christ returns to earth He will be glorified in His people. We will receive glory in Him and from Him (2 Thess. 2:14). On that day, believers will be on display as the objects of His grace, and He will be admired as a result (2 Thess. 1:10). In fact, as sinners saved by grace we will be on display for all eternity that *"in the ages to come he might shew the exceeding riches of his grace in his kindness toward us in Christ Jesus"* (Eph. 2:7).

Fanny Crosby's words ring true today and will do so in eternity:

> *To God be the glory great things He hath done!*
> *So loved He the world that He gave us His Son,*
> *Who yielded His life our redemption to win,*
> *And opened the life-gate that all may go in.*

THE GLORY OF HIS GRACE

Oh, perfect redemption, the purchase of blood,
To every believer the promise of God;
The vilest offender who truly believes,
That moment from Jesus a pardon receives.

Praise the Lord, Praise the Lord, Let the earth hear His voice;
Praise the Lord, Praise the Lord, Let the people rejoice;
O, come to the Father, through Jesus the Son,
And give Him the glory; great things He hath done.

MEDITATIVE THOUGHTS

2 Peter 1:9 says a lack of fruit in the Christian's life is caused by shortsightedness and forgetfulness. Here Peter refers to those who have lost sight of what they have been saved for and forgotten what they have been saved from—the eternal consequences of their sin.

In the physical realm, shortsightedness and forgetfulness are signs of aging. In the spiritual realm, these characteristics are the recipe for an unfruitful life. The root of worship is a sense of awe and wonder at what God has accomplished in saving sinful men and women, and the knowledge of the part we are privileged to play in His eternal plan.

• • •

Revelation 1:5-6 gives a summary of what the Lord Jesus has done for us and how believers should respond. There are three verbs to note: He **loved** us; He **cleansed** us in His own blood; and He **made** us a kingdom of priests. Our response is to give Him glory and dominion both now and forever—glory for His **person** and dominion due to the **position** He occupies.

• • •

In heaven all the redeemed will sing a new song, a song that proclaims the worthiness of the Lamb and gives Him glory (Rev. 5:9). Here and now His own can sing:

> *Salvation's glory all be paid,*
> *To Him who sits upon the throne;*
> *And to the Lamb whose blood was shed;*
> *Thou! Thou art worthy, Thou alone!*

Let us with joy adopt the strain
We soon shall sing forever there:
Worthy's the Lamb for sinners slain,
Worthy alone the crown to wear!

Robert Sandeman

CHAPTER SIX
GIVE GOD GLORY

Earlier chapters have examined God's revealed glory in the Old Testament as the prerequisite for worship and service for God. The last two chapters have presented the glory of our Saviour and the glory of our salvation. This chapter explores the glory of His church and His glory in the church.

So much of church life—certainly in North America and likely beyond—is all about the individual. The unspoken line for many would be, "what's in it for me?" Church life, to a great extent, has become centered on the needs of the individual. This focus is off-balance in that it is more about us than about the Lord Jesus.

Samuel Stone's hymn expresses the preeminence of the Lord Jesus in His church.

> *The Church's one foundation is Jesus Christ Her Lord;*
> *She is His new creation by water and the Word:*
> *From heav'n He came and sought her to be His holy bride;*
> *With His own blood He bought her, and for her life He died.*

The purposes of a local church are varied. There are to be times of fellowship characterized by love and encouragement. There should also be teaching from God's word, times of prayer, and the remembrance of the Lord Jesus (Acts 2:42). Ultimately everything that takes place within a local church should be to His glory. The saints need to be equipped to serve Christ and to grow into His likeness. Believers are to offer up holy sacrifices and show forth His praises together. The corporate life of a Christian is to be more about Him than about "me."

THE GOD OF GLORY

THE PURPOSES OF GOD

Paul ends his prayer in Ephesians 3 with a notable doxology (vv. 20-21). He exults the surpassing power of God, stating that God can do far more than we can ask or think. This power is at work in us. Paul moves on from God's power to the church, and finishes with this thought, *"unto him be glory in the church by Christ Jesus."* God's power works in us yet glory flows to Him from the church.

The context of these verses has to do with the wisdom of God being displayed in the church *"throughout all ages."* God's plan of redemption has resulted in Jew and Gentile being made one, *"that the Gentiles should be fellow heirs, of the same body, and partakers of His promise in Christ through the gospel"* (Eph. 3:6, NKJV).

It was Paul's privilege to preach among the Gentiles *"the unsearchable riches of Christ"* (Eph. 3:8). This is one of the many mysteries revealed in the New Testament which was concealed in the Old Testament. God's plan was that the splendor of this mystery—Jew and Gentile in one body—would display His wisdom to the occupants of the heavenlies (Eph. 3:10). This was the fulfillment of God's eternal purpose that He accomplished in Christ Jesus our Lord.

Ephesians 1:6 states that our individual salvation is to the *"praise of the glory of his grace"* (Eph. 1:6). As a result, individual believers will be on display as objects of His grace for eternity that *"in the ages to come He might show the exceeding riches of His grace"* (Eph. 2:7, NKJV). The glory described in Ephesians 3 refers to the universal body of Christ. This display of glory is not about practice but has everything to do with the outworking of God's purposes. The *"manifold wisdom of God"* (Eph. 3:10), is revealed through the composition of the church. That which was hidden in the past has now been made visible, namely, that Gentiles would be fellow heirs.

The glory of the church is also seen "by" or "in" (J. N. Darby, A. T. Robertson) Christ Jesus. All of the attributes mentioned so far in the epistle of Ephesians are visible in the church and in its Head, Christ Jesus. The love, mercy, grace, wisdom, and power of God are all seen in the institution of the church and in its risen Head.

The angelic world looks on at this and learns of the wisdom of God (Eph. 3:10). They see God's eternal purposes being worked out in Christ. They see the glory of God on display through His body on earth. This display of glory will go beyond time and remain for all eternity.

The church universal is given many names in the New Testament: a holy temple (Eph. 2:21), a spiritual house (1 Pet. 2:5), the household of God (Eph. 2:19), and the church of the living God (1 Tim. 3:15). The church is the habitation of God in the Spirit (Eph. 2:22).

In the Old Testament Tabernacle, the glory of God filled the Holy of Holies. In the New Testament it is the church, a holy temple, in which God resides in the Spirit.

THE PERSON OF CHRIST

The church by its very existence displays the glory of the Lord Jesus. The church is the outcome He anticipated as a result of going to the cross; *"He shall see the labor of His soul, and be satisfied"* (Isa. 53:11). It is a part of the joy that was set before Him which caused Him to endure the cross and despise the shame (Heb. 12:2).

The church is the pearl of great price for which the Lord Jesus sold all that He had in order to buy it (Matt. 13:45-46). A pearl is formed as a result of a wound in the side; it is the only gem stone produced from a living organism. It is the only gem that continues to grow, as long as it is attached to the wounded side. What a fitting metaphor of the church, purchased at great cost and now on display for His glory.

The church is a building but the foundation, the chief cornerstone, and capstone is Christ (1 Pet. 2:7). It is a body with its Head, Jesus Christ, in heaven. It is a bride and He the

THE GOD OF GLORY

heavenly Bridegroom (Rev. 21:9). The church, His body, is the fullness—the compliment and completion—of Him who fills all in all (Eph. 1:23).

Colossians 1 describes the creation of the universe and the formation of the church. Both are a result of the work of the Lord Jesus. The prepositions in verses 16 and 17, *"by,"* *"through,"* and *"for,"* describe His relationship to His creation. Similar prepositions can be applied to Him in relation to the formation of the Church.

Colossians 1:20 tells us that it is *"by Him"* the work of reconciliation was accomplished. In verse 22 it is *"in Him"* and through His death that this reconciling work was made possible and by which He made peace. He is the Head, the Beginning, the Firstborn and in all things He is to have the preeminence (Col. 1:18). Though the word "for" is not used, it is implied due to the position He occupies. Thus it can be said that the church was formed "for Him" and, like the physical creation, the church displays His glory.

Revelation 1:5-6 describes the outcome of the work of the Lord Jesus. He loved us, washed us from our sins, and made us a *"kingdom of priests"* (JND). The outcome is that glory and dominion should be His in time and in eternity. In 1 Peter 2 believers are described collectively as a spiritual house, a holy nation, but also as a holy and royal priesthood. This priesthood is displayed when believers gather together; it functions when spiritual sacrifices are offered up to God and when the gospel goes out to the world.

THE PRACTICES OF THE CHURCH

Individual believers are saved in such a way that all the glory goes to God. There is no merit in us, no work that we can boast about, and no righteousness that we may present. We are bought with a price and as a result we are to glorify God in our bodies (1 Cor. 6:20). Paul said whether we eat or drink, or whatever we do, all should be done to the glory of

God (1 Cor. 10:31). In Galatians 6:14 Paul also wrote, *"God forbid that I should glory, save in the cross of our Lord Jesus Christ."*

Believers should let their light shine through their testimony and good works so that others will see these deeds and glorify God (Matt. 5:16). We are His ambassadors (2 Cor. 5:20), His witnesses, and His brethren; as such our goal is to bring glory to His name. Since this is true in our individual lives, how much more so when we gather together as a local church.

Certain corporate practices are specifically designed to bring glory to God. Corporate worship, by its very nature, is all about God's glory. Worship ascribes worth to the Lord Jesus and lifts up His name to the glory of God. The local church that does not worship misses this opportunity to be occupied with God's glory.

Many debate the interpretation of 1 Corinthians 11:1-16. Opinions abound as to what this passage regarding the practice of headcovering means and how it should be applied. What is clear is that the passage has to do with the headship of Christ and the glory of God. The simplest approach seems to relate directly with our theme of glory. In the passage, everything that speaks of man's glory is to be covered in church gatherings. In contrast, that which displays God's glory is to remain visible. When a woman's head is covered, her glory and the glory of the man are said to be covered. When the man's head remains uncovered, the text tells us that God's glory is visible. We may not understand all the facets of this passage, but it is almost universally accepted that males should not have their heads covered during church gatherings. More such symbolism follows later on in 1 Corinthians 11 with respect to the bread and wine used to remember the Lord Jesus.

1 Corinthians 11:10 says that the angels observe the church as it gathers and they learn lessons about headship. They see God's glory displayed in the uncovered head of the man. This is another way that the universal church shows God's wisdom and the local church displays His glory.

THE GOD OF GLORY

Unity in the local church is to the glory of God. Romans 15:5-6 records Paul's prayer for God to grant his readers like-mindedness. Paul desired unity for the church at Rome so that they may with *"one mind and one mouth glorify God."* Disunity and selfishness put the focus on man and rob God of His glory.

In the Lord's prayer in John 17 the Lord Jesus gives a report of His ministry in fulfilling the Father's will. The Lord said He gave the disciples—and by extension us—gifts from above. Christ gave us eternal life, revealed the Father's name, conveyed the Father's words, and gave us the glory the Father had given Him (John 17:2, 6, 8, 22). John 17:22 says, *"the glory which thou gavest me I have given them; that they may be one, even as we are one."* Thus according to the Lord Jesus' prayer, glory is connected to the unity that exists between the Father and the Son.

How saints are received should also be to God's glory. Believers are to *"receive ye one another, as Christ also received us to the glory of God"* (Rom. 15:7). In practice, believers are often received on our terms rather than how God has accepted them. Care should be exercised not to go beyond the Word of God. To refuse to receive God's people on the basis that He has received them (i.e. by grace) is to deny the unity of the body and to cover His glory.

Even in eternity the church will proclaim the worthiness of God. Many commentators feel that the 24 elders of Revelation 5:8 represent the church in heaven. These elders sing a *"new song,"* a phrase that speaks of the song of the redeemed. Of the five declarations made in chapters 4 and 5 of Revelation, this is the only one specifically called a song. The song starts with a proclamation of the worthiness of the Lamb, the declaration of His glory.

The primary purpose for the church's existence is the glory of the Lord Jesus Christ; it is His Church. This is expressed well in the following hymn by S. Medley:

GIVE GOD GLORY

In Him it is ordained to raise,
a temple to Jehovah's praise,
Composed of all His saints who own,
no Savior but the Living Stone,

How vast the building see it rise,
the work how great the plan how wise!
O wondrous fabric! Power unknown:
that rests it on the Living Stone.

MEDITATIVE THOUGHTS

The Lord Jesus is the head of the body, the church, and He occupies the highest place so that in all things He might have the preeminence. Paul's prayer in Ephesians 3 ends with the desire that the Lord Jesus would receive glory in the church. This is a topic that should concern all believers. How is this accomplished and what part should each one play?

• • •

God's glory is connected to the unity that exists among the Godhead and is displayed in the unity that exists between His children. It is incumbent on believers to endeavor to keep the unity which the Spirit has produced in the bond of peace (Eph. 4:3). The challenge may be put this way: Do I as a believer build walls or bridges? Am I exclusive or inclusive?

• • •

As mentioned earlier, pearls are formed as a result of a wound in the side. Consider that a bride for Adam (Eve) was created the same way. The next prominent bride found in Genesis (Rebekah in chapter 24), was sought by an unnamed servant and brought to the father's house. The final bride in Genesis (Asenath in Genesis 41), a Gentile, is presented to the son of Jacob when he is on the throne.

These brides in Genesis illustrate well the main events in the life of the church: the first has to do with the **formation** of the church; the second with its **furtherance**; and the last with its **future**.

CHAPTER SEVEN

HE SHALL BEAR THE GLORY

The second coming of the Lord Jesus to earth will be different than His first appearance as a babe in a manger. The first coming of Christ was in obscurity and humility. He laid aside the visible display of glory and took upon Himself the form of a servant and the likeness of man. When He returns to earth, He will appear—as He did on the Mount of Transfiguration—shining brighter than the noon day sun. The disciples were promised a glimpse of the kingdom and three of them saw the glory associated with the future reign of Christ. No longer will He be seen as the lowly Man of Sorrows, rather He will be on display as the King of Glory.

The word most often used in the New Testament for this event is *parousia* meaning "appearance and subsequent presence." Theologically the word "revelation" is used to distinguish this visible appearance from the "rapture." At the revelation of Christ every eye will see Him (Rev. 1:7); all the world will behold the Son of Man *"coming in the clouds of heaven with power and great glory"* (Matt. 24:30).

THE GLORY OF HIS PERSON

Titus 2:11-13 references two appearances of the Lord Jesus. In verses 11 and 13 the word rendered *"appeared"* and *"appearing"* in English comes from the Greek word *epiphany* which means "to make visible or to be manifest." In verse 11

THE GOD OF GLORY

we read that **grace** was made visible by the Lord Jesus when He brought salvation to all men. In the Gospels, primarily the Gospel of John, grace is associated with Christ's character and conduct. Here Titus is using personification, a figure of speech which refers to an object or concept as a person.

In verse 13 it is **glory** that is personified in the person of *"our great God and Saviour Jesus Christ"* (JND). *"The blessed hope"* and the *"appearing of the glory"* (JND) are best viewed as applying to the same event. In the same way, Darby links "our great God and Saviour" into one person, referring to Christ. The KJV renders verse 13, *"the great God and our Saviour Jesus Christ."* Darby's translation indicates that, when the Lord Jesus comes to earth again, His **person** will be a manifestation of glory (in contrast with His character and conduct in verse 11).

The scene of Christ's return to earth is described in Revelation 19:11-21. In this passage, the Lord Jesus rides a white horse, His eyes are as a flame of fire, and His robe is dipped in blood. On his robe and thigh a name is written, *"King Of Kings, And Lord Of Lords"* (v. 16). The Lord Himself compared His coming to lightning flashing from the east to the west (Matt. 24:27).

Zechariah 6:9-14 prophesies about this same glory to be revealed when *"the man whose name is The Branch"* is introduced to the world. The complete phrase found in Zechariah 6:12 is also found in John 19:5, *"Behold the man."* In Latin it is the phrase *Ecce Homo*. As the representative of human government in John 19, it was Pilate who said these words. This was the last the world saw of Christ, *"a Man of Sorrows and acquainted with grief"* (Isa. 53:3, NKJV). The Lord Jesus was so disfigured and beaten that the Scripture tells us his form *"was...marred more than any man"* (Isa. 52:14).

When "Behold the man" is heard on earth again, the words will not be spoken by a representative of human government but by Almighty God. The volume will be greater and the audience larger. The response will no longer be, *"We will not have this man to reign over us"* (Luke 19:14). No longer will the Lord Jesus be seen as the lowly Man of Sorrows; He will be presented as the Messiah in all His glory and splendor. The Father says of Him, *"he shall bear the glory"* (Zech. 6:13).

Zechariah presents the Lord Jesus as a priest on His throne. Verse 13 goes on to say that *"the counsel of peace shall be between them both,"* likely meaning that the offices of king and priest will be united in Christ. The silver and gold for the temple will be made into elaborate crowns in anticipation of a crowning day that is coming by and by (v. 11).

It is at this time that all those who come out of the tribulation will bow the knee and acknowledge that Jesus Christ is Lord. The Lord will be King over all the earth and His reign will be glorious. The angels of God will worship Him and the entire universe will proclaim His worthiness when the glory of His person is revealed on earth.

THE GLORY OF HIS POWER

The Lord Jesus will also display the greatness of His power when He returns to earth at His revelation. He will be *"revealed from heaven with his mighty angels, In flaming fire taking vengeance on them that know not God, and that obey not the gospel of our Lord Jesus Christ"* (2 Thess. 1:7-8). It is at this time that the unsaved will be banished from the presence of the Lord and *"the glory of his power"* (v. 9).

Once again, the Lord's "revelation" will be in significant contrast to His first appearance on earth. Isaiah 42:2 expresses the gentleness of the Lord Jesus at His first coming, *"He will not cry out, nor raise His voice"* (NKJV). The passage goes on to speak of His tender dealings with humanity. However, verse 13 of the same chapter says, *"The LORD shall go forth like a mighty man; He shall stir up His zeal like a man of war. He shall cry out, yes, shout aloud; He shall prevail against His enemies"* (NKJV). Two different words are used for the phrase "cry out" in Isaiah 42. The second word means "shall shout mightily" in the Septuagint. In verse 2 *"He will not cry out"* has to do with the Lord's **compassion,** whereas *"cry out"* in verse 13 has to do with His **conquest.**

In Isaiah 63 the Lord Jesus is pictured as coming from Edom as the One who treads in the winepress of the wrath of God. Verse 1 says, *"this that is glorious in his apparel, travelling in the greatness of his strength."* The rest of the chapter goes on to speak of the Lord's fury, anger, and vengeance as He executes judgement on the earth.

The "man of sin" will experience defeat in a singular way when Christ comes again to the earth. The Lord Jesus will consume the "son of perdition" with the breath of His mouth and destroy "the lawless one" with the brightness of His coming (2 Thess. 2:8). This beast and the false prophet will be cast alive into the lake of fire.

The sight of the Lord Jesus' coming will be spectacular. Referring back to Revelation 19, we remember that He will come riding a white horse, His head will be crowned with many crowns, and He will be clothed in a robe dipped in blood. A sharp sword will come out of His mouth with which He will strike the nations. The armies that gather to wage war against Him will be destroyed by that sword, the spoken Word of God.

Joel pictures these nations gathered in the "valley of decision" or the "valley of Jehoshaphat" (more commonly known to us as the "plains of Megiddo"). The Lord will come in judgement on these nations because their wickedness is great. He will roar and cry out and the *"heavens and the earth shall shake"* (Joel 3:16) in response. When His feet touch the Mount of Olives, the mount will be split in two and a valley will be formed. The glory of the Lord's power will be revealed through these victorious displays of His overwhelming might.

THE GLORY OF HIS PEOPLE

Every believer looks forward to the rapture of the church with anticipation, but our hope also extends to the revelation of Jesus Christ at His second coming to earth. Our hope is tied to His glory, both seeing it and sharing in it.

Collectively the church, the bride of Christ, will be presented to Him as *"a glorious church, not having spot, or wrinkle"* (Eph. 5:27). When He appears for us, our bodies will be changed from these earthly bodies to be made like His glorious body. Not only does the gospel guarantee the forgiveness of our sins, but also that believers will share in the glory of our Lord Jesus. The Lord's prayer in John 17 includes the request that those given to Him might be with Him and see His glory. Jude 24 reminds us that believers will be presented *"faultless before the presence of his glory with exceeding joy."*

The whole creation is groaning in anticipation of the day when it will enter into the glorious liberty prepared for the children of God (Rom. 8:21). It will be at the second coming that the church, the bride of Christ, is presented to the world in dazzling splendor. She is identified with the holy city that comes down from heaven having the very glory of God (Rev. 21:2).

2 Thessalonians 1:10 says that the Lord Jesus will be glorified in His saints. What is amazing is the fact that He will be glorified in us, for we are but sinners saved by grace and clothed in His righteousness.

THE GLORY OF HIS PEACE

When the Lord Jesus returns to establish His kingdom, there will finally be peace on earth. This peace is connected to His person and presence. Jesus Christ is the One of whom Jacob spoke so long ago, *"Shiloh,"* the One who is peace (Gen. 49:10). He is the *"Prince of Peace"* referred to in Isaiah 9:6. Micah 5:5 says of Him, *"this man shall be the peace."* Melchizedek was a type of the Lord Jesus in Genesis 14 because he was not only the king of righteousness but the king of peace as well.

God's message to Haggai tells us that the glory of the millennial temple will be greater than that of the former temple. *"And in this place will I give peace, saith the LORD of hosts"* (Hag.

2:9). The reign of the Lord Jesus will be characterized—as never before seen on earth—by the glory of His peace.

"The earth will be filled with the knowledge of the glory of the LORD as the waters cover the sea" (Hab. 2:14, NKJV). The Lord will rule over the nations with a rod of iron (Rev. 19:15), but that rule will be in righteousness and truth (Zech. 8:8). All the nations will come to Jerusalem to worship the King, the Lord of hosts. When He enters the city, the question will be asked, *"Who is this King of glory?"* The response will be, *"The LORD of hosts, he is the King of glory"* (Ps. 24:10). The very name of the city will be changed to "Jehovah Shammah" which means *"The LORD is there"* (Ezek. 48:35).

Psalm 72 ends with these words about the reign of Christ, *"And blessed be his glorious name for ever: and let the whole earth be filled with his glory"* (v. 19). Every believer can heartily respond, *"Amen. Even so, come, Lord Jesus"* (Rev. 22:20).

MEDITATIVE THOUGHTS

The feasts and holidays that the Lord ordained are very different than those established by various nations, cultures, or religions. All special commemorative days either look back to a significant event or are the response to current events. The occasions God designated not only look to the **past**, they also touch the **present** and involve a future **prospect**.

An example of this can be seen in the Passover. The Passover looked back to God freeing the Israelites from Egypt and was also a present reminder of God's redemption. Furthermore, it anticipated the future death of Christ as the Passover Lamb.

The Lord's Supper is a similar institution. It is observed in remembrance of Christ's sacrifice. It shows forth His death and encourages His people to deeper devotion. Yet it also anticipates His return in that it is to be celebrated *"till he come"* (1 Cor. 11:26).

• • •

It is sometimes—maybe often—discouraging to consider the moral condition of our society. Many believers feel that better leadership would lead to positive change in the moral climate. However, it is unreasonable to expect unrighteous people to act in a righteous way. Such behavior is contrary to their nature. Only when the Lord Jesus comes to reign in righteousness, perfect justice, and truth will the moral fabric of society be forever transformed for the good of all. It will not happen until He occupies the throne.

• • •

The "Branch" is a Messianic title that possibly comes from the same root word as does "Nazareth." Six Old Testament passages make mention of this description of the Messiah: Isaiah 4 and 11, Jeremiah 23 and 33, and Zechariah 3 and 6. In these chapters four different descriptions of the Branch are given. Isaiah 4:2 says, *"In that day shall the branch of the LORD be beautiful and glorious."* In Isaiah 11, Jeremiah 23 and 33, the Messiah is referred to as a Branch out of Jesse and David. In Zechariah 3:8 we read, *"my servant the Branch,"* and in Zechariah 6:12 we find, *"Behold the man whose name is The BRANCH."* These descriptions present the Lord Jesus as King (Matthew), as Servant (Mark), as Man (Luke), and as Lord (John).

• • •

These words penned by Isaac Watts will ring true in the coming day of Christ's reign. This hymn contains far more verses than in our hymnbooks and even more than are recorded here:

Jesus shall reign where'er the sun
Does his successive journeys run;
His kingdom stretch from shore to shore
Till moons shall wax and wane no more.

People and realms of every tongue
Dwell on His love with sweetest song;
And infant voices shall proclaim
Their early blessings on His Name.

The scepter well becomes His hands;
All Heav'n submits to His commands;
His justice shall avenge the poor,
And pride and rage prevail no more.

The saints shall flourish in His days,
Dressed in the robes of joy and praise;

*Peace, like a river, from His throne
Shall flow to nations yet unknown.*

CHAPTER EIGHT
TO GOD BE THE GLORY

The Scriptures exhort believers, *"Give unto the Lord the glory due unto his name: bring an offering, and come into his courts. O worship the Lord in the beauty of holiness"* (Ps. 96:8-9). Even when the word "glory" is not explicitly referenced, Scripture calls us to render to God His worth or what He is due. The Psalmist directed these verses to Israel but they are applicable to us as well, *"The LORD is great in Zion, And He is high above all the peoples. Let them praise Your great and awesome name—He is holy...Exalt the Lord our God, And worship at His footstool—He is holy"* (Ps. 99:2-3, 5, NKJV).

In heaven worship is given to God and to the Lamb. The new song found in the book of Revelation proclaims that the Lamb is worthy to open the book of seven seals. The next stanza says, *"Worthy is the Lamb who was slain to receive power and riches and wisdom, and strength and honor and glory and blessing!"* (Rev. 5:12, NKJV).

It is the privilege of believers today to enter into the occupation of heaven, that is, to magnify the Lord. The **walk** and **work** as well as the **worship** of a believer should be to God's glory. In contrast, Herod was struck dead specifically because he did not give glory to God (Acts 12:23).

J. S. Bach said, "All music should have no other end and aim than the glory of God and the soul's refreshment; where this is not remembered there is no real music but only a devilish hub-bub."

THE GOD OF GLORY

Bach headed his compositions "J.J." short for "Jesus, Juva" which means "Jesus, help me." He ended them "S.D.G." or "*Soli Dei gratia*" which means "To God alone the praise."[12]

THE GLORY OF OUR WALK

The New Testament makes many references to the believer's "walk," that is, the course or direction of one's life. This walk (or lifestlye) can and should bring glory to God. Believers are exhorted to walk worthy of our calling, in love, in light, and in wisdom. Scripture tells us that those in Christ Jesus are to do good works which God prepared in advance for us to do (Eph. 2:10). *"Christ was raised up from the dead by the glory of the Father, even so we also should walk in newness of life"* (Rom. 6:4).

"Whether you eat or drink, or whatever you do, do all to the glory of God" (1 Cor. 10:31, NKJV). Individuals can choose to be motivated by a desire to do things for self-fulfilment or to bring glory to God. The believer's lifestyle of bringing glory to God should extend to the workplace. *"And whatsoever ye do, do it heartily, as to the Lord, and not unto men…for ye serve the Lord Christ"* (Col. 3:23-24).

J. Boyd Nicholson penned these words:

> *"What do I really desire in this life,*
> *Is it something for me and a little for Thee?*
> *To what do I grandly aspire in the strife?*
> *Is it Thee, my God, is it Thee?*
>
> *What drives me onward to serve day by day?*
> *Is it something for me or glory for Thee?*
> *What motive enlivens each nerve in the fray?*
> *Is it Thee, my God, is it Thee?*

All believers are ambassadors for Christ. According to 2 Corinthians 5:20, we are His representatives on earth during His absence. Paul's words are clear, *"He died for all, that those*

---

12 J. Stowell, *Kingdom Conflict*, (Wheaton: Victor Books, 1985), 77.

who live should no longer live for themselves, but for Him who died for them and rose again" (2 Cor. 5:15, NKJV). *"If anyone is in Christ, he is a new creation...For He made Him who knew no sin to be sin for us, that we might become the righteousness of God in Him"* (2 Cor. 17, 21, NKJV).

The promises God has given us are confirmed and certain in Christ. As those promises are claimed and lived out in a believer's life, it is to the glory of God through us (2 Cor. 1:20).

THE GLORY OF OUR WORK

Paul's letter to Titus places emphasis on the believer carrying out good works. The letter to Titus declares that the Lord saved us to *"purify unto himself a peculiar people, zealous of good works"* (Tit. 2:14). The practical outworking of salvation is that believers are *"to be ready to every good work"* (Tit. 3:1) and are to be careful *"to maintain good works"* (Tit. 3:8, 14).

Matthew 5:16 tells us that our light is to shine in such a way that, when our good work is seen, people will give glory or praise to our Father in heaven. The Lord Jesus' Sermon on the Mount in Matthew 6 emphasized that charity, prayer, and fasting are to be carried out so as not to attract attention to the individual. 2 Corinthians 4:15 expresses the same idea, *"For all things are for your sakes, that grace, having spread through the many, may cause thanksgiving to abound to the glory of God"* (NKJV). Paul is explaining that the suffering experienced in life is for the good of God's people and for the glory of God.

Giving and the administration of finances should also be done to the glory of God. In 2 Corinthians 8, we read that the Macedonians gave sacrificially, out of their deep poverty, but that they first gave themselves to the Lord. The Macedonians' gift was collected by Paul and his companions and administered to the glory of God. Upon delivery it would supply the needs of the saints and cause thanksgiving to be made to God. How funds are handled, forwarded, and ultimately received is important and gives us opportunity to bring glory to God.

THE GLORY OF OUR WORSHIP

On a number of occasions in the New Testament, believers are reminded that glory is ascribed to the Father. For example, Philippians 4:20 reads, *"Now unto God and our Father be glory for ever and ever."* We are also exhorted to give glory to the Son, *"To him be glory both now and for ever. Amen"* (2 Pet. 3:18). These two perspectives fulfill the words of the Lord Jesus, *"that all men should honour the Son, even as they honour the Father"* (John 5:23).

A. W. Tozer called worship the missing jewel. So much of "church life" today is focused on the individual. In many cases, people occupy a pew and are entertained or ministered to without an opportunity to respond. There is little appreciation of the fact that the highest goal of a believer is to worship, giving God glory. Worship is often relegated to a time of singing where those involved may be worshipping but are more likely praising the Lord.

The Lord Jesus told the woman at the well that the Father is seeking worshippers. The Lord went on to say that worship must be performed in spirit and in truth. Worship is not of the flesh nor is it left to the imagination of man. Worship is the conscious response of an individual to who God is based on a revelation from God. Mary's words in her Magnificat embody worship, *"My soul doth magnify the Lord"* (Luke 1:46). The word "magnify" is also included in the margin as being translated "declares the greatness of."

An Old Testament example of worship would be Joseph's words to his brothers in Genesis 45:13, *"tell my father of all my glory...and of all that ye have seen."* The revelation that preceded Joseph's request was that *"God hath made me lord of all..."* (Gen. 45:9). In order to glorify the Son, believers need to tell the Father of the glory of the One who has been made Lord of all, the beloved Son, in whom the Father is well pleased.

As evidenced by the glimpses found in the book of Revelation, the primary occupation of heaven will be to worship the Lamb. Some, perhaps many, will feel a sense of culture shock when they realize that heaven is not all about us but all about Him. There is a day coming when all of the universe will bow the knee and every tongue will confess that Jesus Christ is Lord to the glory of God (Phil. 2:10-11).

GOD'S GLORY AND FRUITFULNESS

In John 15 the Lord Jesus refers to Himself as the true Vine and individual believers as the branches. This extended metaphor has to do with producing fruit as the branches abide in the vine. Verse 8 says that the Father is glorified when believers produce much fruit. Fruit cannot be manufactured, however; it is produced rather as a result of the life in the vine. This is an apt description of what is produced in believers as a result of attachment to Christ. Fruit never attracts attention to itself and it is always for the benefit of others.

Fruit is primarily a matter of character as the Holy Spirit reproduces in the believer the **character** of Christ (Gal. 5:22-23). The Spirit's inner work is then made outwardly visible in our **walk, work**, and **worship**. Fruit is described in relation to **conduct, charity, conversation,** and **converts**. Because fruit is a result of the work of the Spirit of God, it results in the Father being glorified.

MEDITATIVE THOUGHTS

Psalm 113 calls God's people to bless His name—to speak well of Him. The Psalmist writes, *"the Lord is high above all nations, and his glory above the heavens"* (v. 4). There are three stanzas in this psalm. In the first, the exhortation is for the servants of the Lord to bless His name. In the second stanza, God is presented in majesty and humility, humbling Himself to behold the things that are in the heavens and in the earth. The final stanza relates what God has done for us in bringing us out of the ash heap and into fellowship.

In the first stanza, our response of worship is commanded or demanded. In the second, it is the desire of the heart of God that we respond to Him. In the third is found our response to what He has done in lifting us out of the dust and the ash heap. John Phillips gives this outline for Psalm 113: the Lord demands, desires, and deserves our praise.

• • •

The first four letters of the word "doxology" come from the Greek word for glory. Doxology means to give God glory or praise. When used with a definite article, "the Doxology" refers to a hymn of praise that begins, "Praise God from Whom all blessings flow."

• • •

Psalm 8 outlines a spiritual response to the consideration of God's glory. The Psalmist looks up and sees God's glory in the expanse of the universe, recognizing the greatness of God's person and purposes. David's response is to put everything in perspective, *"What is man that You are mindful of him, and the son of man that You visit him?"* (Ps. 8:4, NKJV). It draws from his lips praise to Jehovah his Master, *"how excellent is Your name in all the earth!"* (v. 9, NKJV). Contemplation of God's glory will do these two things in us: put our lives in proper perspective, and produce praise from our lips toward God.

APPENDIX
SERMON OUTLINES

As indicated in the introductory pages, this manuscript is not intended to be an exhaustive study of the God of glory. It will take the endless days of eternity to fully explore the depths of God's glorious nature and to appreciate all that has been granted to the believer as a result of Christ's atoning sacrifice.

As we await His return, we praise the Lord for the revelation of the Word of God. The glimpses of glory that we see therein merely whet our appetite for more of Him.

Because there is so much more to be discovered in the Scriptures with respect to the God of glory, included here are a number of possible sermon outlines for those exercised to dig deeper:

SYNOPSIS of GLORY SERMON OUTLINES

HIS GLORY CAN BE SEEN
In Creation
In Revelation
In Incarnation
In Redemption
In Salvation
In Identification
In Expectation

THE GOD OF GLORY

GLORY AND THE REIGN OF CHRIST
His Parousia
His People
His Presence
His Power
His Peace
His Preeminence

GOD'S GLORY AS SEEN IN THE CHURCH
By its Practices
By its Preaching
By its Praise
By its Proclamation

GLORY BELONGS TO GOD ALONE
His Power declares it
His Person deserves it
His Purpose demands it

GOD'S GLORY AS SEEN IN CHRIST
In His Character
In His Conduct
In His Conversation
In His Conquest

CHRIST'S GLORY IN JOHN'S GOSPEL
His Pre-Incarnate glory
His Personal or Moral glory
His Power in action
His Passion and the glory of the Cross
His Positional or acquired glories
His Present glories

BIBLIOGRAPHY

This bibliography is not complete as many books were consulted for input on particular verses or passages and are not listed here. It is doubtful that any of the material in this book is original; thoughts were gathered from sermons, conversations, and numerous books read over many years. Some of the content was from memory, some from notes in my Bible, and others from sermons I have given. In this day and age, the Internet is of value for comments on verses, definitions, and the studies others have posted.

The books listed here are either on the topic of the glory of God or are theological and technical.

Lancelot C. L. Brenton, *The Septuagint Version: Greek and English* (Grand Rapids: Zondervan Publishing House, 1970)

John W. de Silva, *My Lord and My God* (Kilmarnock: John Ritchie, 2003)

Millard J. Erickson, *Christian Theology* (Grand Rapids, Michigan: Baker Book House, 1983)

Michael P. Green, *Illustrations for Biblical Preaching* (Grand Rapids: Baker Book House, 1989)

Ronald F. Hogan, *The God of Glory* (Neptune: Loizeaux Brothers, 1984)

A. T. Robertson, *Word Pictures in the New Testament.* (Nashville: Broadman Press, 1932)

Charles C. Ryrie, *Transformed by His Glory* (Wheaton: Victor Books, 1990)

Stephens, *The Englishman's Greek New Testament; Giving the Greek Text of Stephens 1550,* Third Edition (London: Samuel Bagster and Sons, Ltd., 1986)

W. E. Vine, *An Expository Dictionary of New Testament Words* (London: Pickering and Inglis, 1939)

WHAT'S UP WITH WORSHIP
GARY McBRIDE

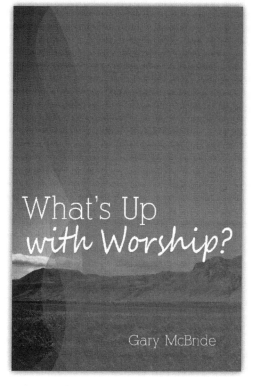

In this volume the author highlights the importance of worship and the "Worship Meeting." There are challenges made to conventional thinking, concerns expressed about current trends, and counsel given with regard to changing tactics. The Lord's people are called to devotion and discipline, to examine and evaluate, and to wonder and worship.

This work draws the distinction between the Lord's Table and the Lord's Supper, between a local church with worship at the core and one that has a pulpit at the center. Most of all it is about the exaltation of the Lord Jesus Christ with a call to *"worship and bow down...kneel before the LORD our Maker"* (Ps. 95:6).

Available from Gospel Folio Press

A STUDY OF FIRST THESSALONIANS: THE MODEL CHURCH
GARY McBRIDE

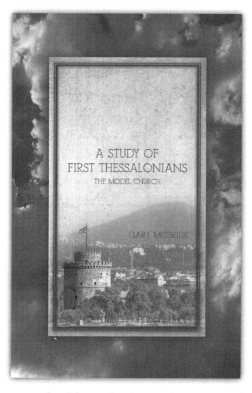

The letter to the Thessalonians educates and exhorts us. All believers want to be in a model church - but what would that look like?

In this book, the author examines 1 Thessalonians to determine what constitutes a Model Church showing that it is not size or structure, not facilities or finances. Instead the Lord commends these believers for their character, conduct and conversation. Other characteristics of a church God commends are: a passion for the lost, a visible love for one another, and a walk that pleases God. The Thessalonians were a model for others in their day and for us today.

Available from Gospel Folio Press